# The Ipswich to Stowmarket
# John Rennie's first can

## Map Key

| | |
|---|---|
| A' Roads | ▬▬▬ |
| 'B' Roads | ▬▬▬ |
| Railway | ▬▬▬ |
| River Gipping | ▬▬▬ |
| Locks | ⌃ |
| Towpath | ▬▬▬ |

**Stowmarket** — Railway Station

A14

Stowupland Lock

B1113

Badley Lock

Needham Lock
Bosmere Lock

**Needham Market** — Railway Station

Creeting Lock

Pipps Ford Lock

Baylham Lock

Shamford Lock

Blakenham Lock

**Great Blakenham**

Claydon Lock
(Lost in the construction of the A14)

Paper Mill Lock

**RIVER GIPPING**
TRUST

Bramford Lock

Sproughton Lock

**Ipswich**

Chantry Lock

Handford Sea Lock — Railway Station — Docks

A14

A12

A14

River Orwell estuary

Map showing the route of the Ipswich to Stowmarket Navigation and the location of the 15 locks that were needed to overcome the height difference between Stowmarket and Ipswich (90 feet / 27.5 metres).

The Navigation is 16 miles long.

0    1    2    3

Miles

Dedicated to the memory of Les Howard
a greatly missed friend and trustee

# A brief history of the river Gipping

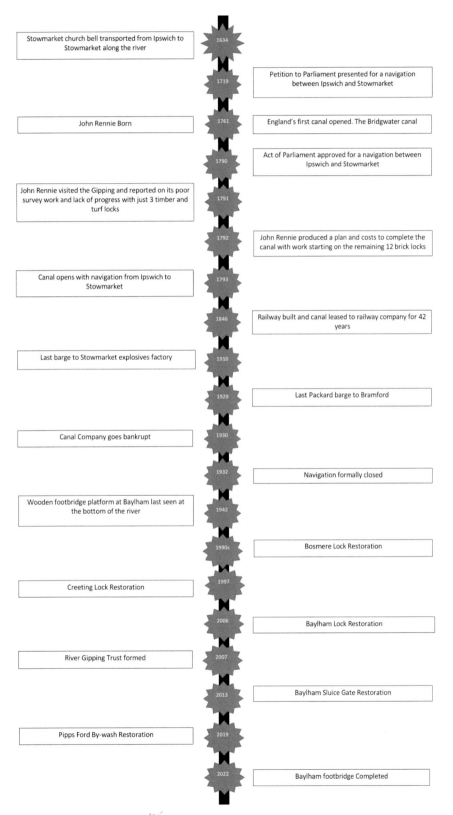

Stowmarket church bell transported from Ipswich to Stowmarket along the river — 1634

1719 — Petition to Parliament presented for a navigation between Ipswich and Stowmarket

John Rennie Born — 1761

1761 — England's first canal opened. The Bridgwater canal

1790 — Act of Parliament approved for a navigation between Ipswich and Stowmarket

John Rennie visited the Gipping and reported on its poor survey work and lack of progress with just 3 timber and turf locks — 1791

1792 — John Rennie produced a plan and costs to complete the canal with work starting on the remaining 12 brick locks

Canal opens with navigation from Ipswich to Stowmarket — 1793

1846 — Railway built and canal leased to railway company for 42 years

Last barge to Stowmarket explosives factory — 1910

1929 — Last Packard barge to Bramford

Canal Company goes bankrupt — 1930

1932 — Navigation formally closed

Wooden footbridge platform at Baylham last seen at the bottom of the river — 1942

1990s — Bosmere Lock Restoration

Creeting Lock Restoration — 1997

2006 — Baylham Lock Restoration

River Gipping Trust formed — 2007

2013 — Baylham Sluice Gate Restoration

Pipps Ford By-wash Restoration — 2019

2022 — Baylham footbridge Completed

RIVER GIPPING
TRUST

# Introduction

The river Gipping was canalised in the 1790s with 15 locks built. In the days before rivers like the Gipping were converted, many of our Inland rivers were already being used to transport raw materials, such as coal, limestone and timber. These stretches of navigable rivers were known as navigations. The Gipping was a navigation many years before it was canalised, but until it was canalised it could only be used when the river levels were perfect.

Men called Navigators dug out the canalised sections of the navigation by hand, in later years this name was shortened to Navvies. It is believed the workforce employed during the Ipswich to Stowmarket Navigation construction was around 200. Most of these men would have been Navigators.

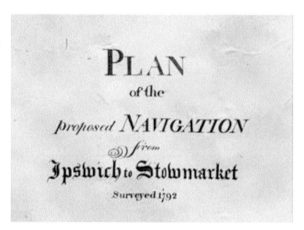

The River Gipping in Suffolk rises from a small spring near the radio mast at Mendlesham but it gets its name from the village of Gipping close by. It is joined by several small streams and the River Rat just below Stowmarket. From Stowmarket it flows down 16 miles towards Ipswich into the tidal River Orwell. Stowmarket is 90 feet (27.5m) above Ipswich.

It is reasonable to assume that the River Gipping was used by the Romans to supply the settlement of Combretovium near Baylham. It was certainly navigable in AD860 when the Danes used it to establish the village of Ratesdana (Rattlesden).

In 1634, the river was used to transport one of the bells of Stowmarket church from Ipswich after it had been recast. The first proposal for the construction of a canal between Ipswich and Stowmarket was in 1719, but the traders of Ipswich objected, fearing loss of trade.

Work started to convert the river into a canal in 1790 with the construction of 15 locks starting at the Ipswich end. The navigation to Stowmarket was expected to be completed within a year, but they soon ran into legal problems with trespassing, resulting in dismissals of key personnel, extra costs and the stoppage of construction work.

One year after starting work only three locks and around two miles of river had been completed, all at the Stowmarket end.

John Rennie was called in to sort out the problems. His involvement began in 1791 and the fifteen lock, sixteen-mile canal was opened a little over 18 months after his initial surveys. The experience helped to develop his expertise and early reputation in bridge and canal engineering.

The Ipswich to Stowmarket navigation (owned by the Stowmarket Navigation Company) was almost certainly the first canal project to be constructed under John Rennie's design and direction on his own account as a consulting engineer.

John Rennie was one of Britain's greatest engineers and after the Ipswich to Stowmarket navigation, went on to design many canals and bridges including the Kennet and Avon canal, both Waterloo and London bridges (the one relocated to USA), London's East India and West India docks, Chatham dockyard and Bell Rock Lighthouse. He was buried at London's St Paul's Cathedral.

Some of the remaining locks and bridges along the River Gipping which were constructed as part of this project are most probably the oldest John Rennie designs still in existence. Of the fifteen locks built, fourteen lock chambers remain with water flowing through them.

The River Gipping Trust aims to restore and improve the towpath alongside the river and reinstate limited navigation to enable and encourage leisure pursuits to aid well-being, increase biodiversity and preserve its historic heritage.

Since the river Gipping was canalised in 1793 it has often been referred to by quite a few different names. Newspapers in the mid 1850s seemed to mostly refer to it as the river Gipping. But around the turn of the century it was often referred to as being a canal. In 1906, the Ipswich Star referred to it as a canal and the 'Gipping Canal' in its editorial. In 1907, they suggested that the "canal between Stowmarket and Ipswich should be restored". In 1979, John Marriage, the well respected Essex historian, referred to it as the Gipping Navigation - as being its more usual title. More recently it has been called the Stowmarket Navigation. The navigation company was called the Stowmarket Navigation Company. In this book we have generally referred to it as the Ipswich to Stowmarket Navigation, as this seems to best reflect the historic heritage of the then navigable river.

# Contents

# 1. Who was John Rennie and how did he get involved with a river in Suffolk?

One year into the construction of the canal, the Trustees of the Stowmarket Navigation Company asked the Scotsman John Rennie, (1761-1821) to review the project's lack of progress. Following his inspection at the end of 1791, he advised that the original survey of the river was inadequate, inaccurate and recommended a new survey.

John Rennie by Henry Raeburn - www.ice.org.uk

John Rennie was a world leading civil engineer, known for pioneering ideas and an unerring ability to drive projects to completion. His diverse range of work included bridges, canals, fen drainage, river navigations, docks and harbours. He was frequently called upon to adjudicate on the design work of his contemporaries.

Originally trained as a millwright in Scotland, Rennie worked for James Watt in 1784 before setting up his own business in Blackfriars, London, in 1791. He started surveying and planning canals and was commissioned to survey the Basingstoke Canal for William Jessop. This led to his involvement in the Ipswich to Stowmarket Navigation, which is thought to have been his first canal project.

Following the Ipswich to Stowmarket Navigation, Rennie moved on to work on the Lancaster Canal in 1792, the Chelmer and Blackwater Canal, Essex, in 1793, the Kennet and Avon Canal, Wiltshire, in 1794 and the Scottish Crinan Canal in 1794.

In 1800, he was appointed engineer to the London Docks and in 1803, engineer to the East India Docks.

He later designed famous road bridges including Waterloo Bridge, Southwark Bridge and London Bridge over the Thames. Others across the country, included Kelso, Scotland which acted as a model for Waterloo Bridge. For many years he was engaged in extensive drainage operations in the Lincolnshire and Norfolk fens.

London Bridge 1900s

Nathalie Chevalier, Victorianweb.org

Rennie was born on 7 June 1761, near East Linton, 20 miles east of Edinburgh, the ninth child of a tenant farmer. This was the same year the Bridgewater Canal opened, which heralded the start of the canal boom that was to revo-lutionise industrial transport in England.

When John Rennie was a student at Edinburgh, he impressed a visiting Mathew Boulton. This connection gave Rennie his first important job as the London agent for Boulton & Watt, the world's premier steam engine manufacturers, supervising the installation of a steam engine at Albion Mill in London. Aged 29, Rennie moved from mechanical to civil engineering, earning a reputation for canals, bridges, docks and lighthouses. He married Martha Ann Mackintosh in 1790 (d.1806), They had seven children. John Rennie was an imposing figure, 6ft 4in tall, and 15 stone who suffered badly from rheumatism. By contemporary accounts, Rennie lived to work, and had few other interests. He died, after a short illness, at his house in Stamford Street, London, on 4 October 1821, and was buried in the crypt at St. Paul's Cathedral.

His two sons became successful engineers, George as a mechanical engineer, John as a civil engineer. Both sons helped complete several of their father's projects after his death. His son, Sir John Rennie became the third president of the Institution of Civil Engineers in 1845. In October 2021, the Institution of Civil Engineers commemorated John Rennie's death 200 years ago and included his probable first ever canal project, the Stowmarket Navigation in The Life and Works of John Rennie (7 June 1761 – 4 October 1821).
https://rbt.org.uk/john-rennie/projects/stowmarket-navigation-2/
https://rbt.org.uk/john-rennie/

# 2. The River Gipping – Early Years

Alongside the river at Baylham is the site of the important Roman fort and settlement of Combretovium. This town was on the main road north from Colchester which led into the heart of Iceni country, famous for the rebellion led by Queen Boudicca, who was based at Thetford. There were five Roman roads leading into Combretovium, from Norwich, Colchester, Long Melford, Framlingham and Peasenhall. During the Roman occupation of Britain, Coddenham / Baylham was the largest settlement in Suffolk.

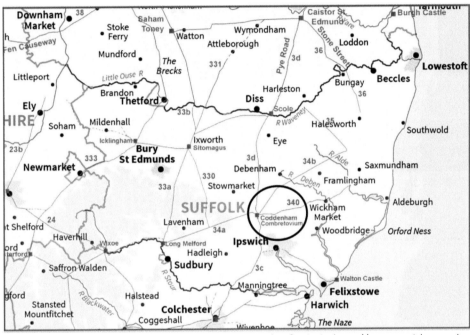

David Ratledge – Travelling with the Roman Roads of Britain http://www.twithr.co.uk

The fort site lies alongside the river on the south side of Mill Lane around the Baylham Rare Breeds Farm. Excavations indicated an earlier small fort, which was replaced by a larger one. The larger fort encloses 14.5 acres and its defences include a triple ditch system. The smaller fort of 5.3 acres lies within this and is surrounded by a set of four ditches.

The fort defended an important road junction and was crucial to the Roman control of the Iceni region. Now little evidence of this remains, other than artefacts displayed in museums. The British Museum holds a double bronze mirror, 2.5 inches in diameter, with the head of Nero on one side and a general addressing soldiers on the other. Other artefacts are held by the Ipswich Museum, Colchester Museum and some at the Baylham Rare Breeds Farm.

There is evidence that the river was navigable as far back as AD860 when the Danes used it to establish a camp in the village that is now known as Rattlesden. The village is referred to in the Domesday Book as Ratlesdena, and Rachestdena and Rastedena. These names derive from "rates" meaning boat and "doenas" meaning Danes. The Saxon Chronicles for AD866 state: "This year ….. came a large heathen army into England and fixed their winter-quarters in East- Anglia, where they were soon horsed; and the inhabitants made peace with them".

The area features again in the Anglo-Saxon chronicles in reference to AD991: "This year was Ipswich plundered; and very soon afterwards was Alderman Britnoth slain at Maidon. In this same year it was resolved that tribute should be given, for the first time, to the Danes, for the great terror they occasioned by the sea-coast". Following the Viking victory at the Battle of Maldon, Æthelred was advised by Sigeric the Serious, Archbishop of Canterbury, to buy peace with a bribe of 10,000 Roman pounds (3,300 kg) of silver. This money, later known as Danegelt, was not effective because the Vikings raided the Ipswich area again in AD993 and AD1010.

It has been suggested that Caen stone was brought from Normandy, up the Orwell and then to Bury St-Edmunds to rebuild the Abbey over the period 1070 to 1095, but it is now thought that the stone came from Barnack in Northamptonshire.

In 1567, Sir Thomas Gresham built the 'Burse' in Cornhill, London, later renamed the Royal Exchange by Queen Elizabeth in 1570. Timber for the roof came from Sir Thomas's estate at Ringshall. Trees were taken to Battisford Tye common and sawpits dug out in order to cut the timber for the roof framework that was taken by boat to London.

The town of Ipswich dates from the 6th century as an Anglo-Saxon settlement at the natural Ford at the lower end of the Gipping. The old name, Gippeswick combines the name of the river and "-wich" used as a term in Anglo-Saxon England for settlements. By the time of the Domesday Book, there were two bridges crossing a natural peninsula that separated the busy trading port of Gipswich (Ipswich) from Over Stoke.

In 1634, the river was used to transport one of the bells of Stowmarket church from Ipswich after it had been recast. This particular bell weighed 5 cwt. (250kgs). In 1719, there was an attempt to make the river navigable when the chief inhabitants of Stowmarket, including Justices of the Peace, gentlemen, tradesmen and freeholders, petitioned Parliament for a navigation. This was blocked by the Ipswich Corporation, who thought it would be detrimental to their town.

# 3. Canal Plans Prior to John Rennie's involvement

In 1789, six local gentlemen engaged William Jessop, to survey the valley to provide proposals for a navigation. Jessop was a well-known and respected canal engineer who had taken over from his old master, John Smeaton, as the leading canal engineer of the day.

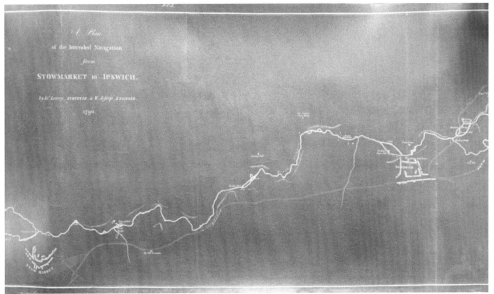

Stowmarket to Needham Market Sections

A survey made by Isaac Lenny, a surveyor from Norwich, endorsed by Jessop, led to an Act being passed in April 1790. This authorised works on the river from Stowupland Bridge, Stowmarket, to Handford Bridge, Ipswich and the upgrading of the River Orwell between Handford Bridge and Stoke Bridge in Ipswich. An additional lateral cut in Stowmarket to the turnpike road was never made.

The Act appointed six trustees who were empowered to borrow an initial £14,300 and raise a further £6,000 by mortgaging the property, if required.

The waterway, including the towpath, was to be no more than 18 yards wide, or 20 yards at winding places or where the banks were more than three feet high. An unusual clause in the Act prohibited the carrying of fishing tackle by boats using the navigation, for which a fine of £5 could be charged.

The first meeting of the new company took place on 19 April 1790, and Jessop was asked to prepare drawings which would form the basis for tenders.

On 7 June 1790, the directors appointed James Smith from Reading as surveyor, at a salary of £300. They expected the navigation to be finished by October 1791 when Smith's contract ended.

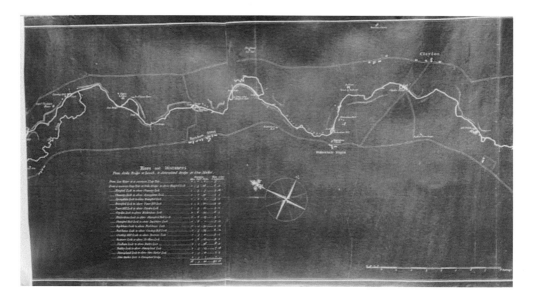

Needham Market to Claydon Section with rises and distances

At the same meeting, they appointed Mr Baynes of Stowmarket to handle legal matters. Dyson and Pinkerton were appointed as contractors; both were members of civil engineering families who had collaborated on a number of schemes since the 1760s.

John Dyson Sr had worked with James Pinkerton on the Adlingfleet Drainage scheme, the Driffield Navigation and the Laneham Drainage scheme, but for this project, he worked with George Pinkerton, thought to be one of James' younger sons.

William Jessop's plan was for a navigation with locks being made from turf and timber. Work started in 1790 at the Ipswich end of the navigation, but there were problems. Baynes was sacked after less than a month, because of "unaccommodating and improper behaviour", and in October Dyson and Pinkerton were dismissed for trespassing on land which did not belong to the Trustees. Legal action caused delays and extra costs, though some work carried on during the lawsuit.

Smith set up a brickworks in January 1791, and a contract to build six locks was awarded to Samuel Wright, millwright of Ipswich, in June.

Because of the dispute, all work stopped at the Ipswich end preventing the transport of materials up the navigation, the overland route was used instead to enable work on the Stowmarket end to continue.

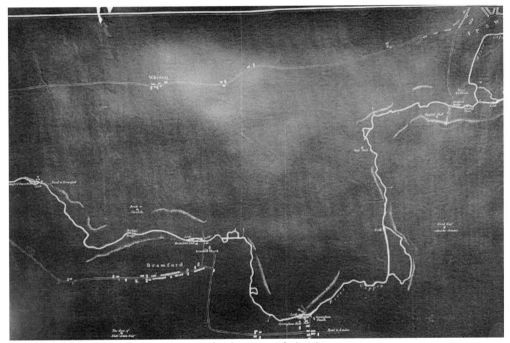

Bramford to Ipswich Section

On 14 November 1791 the dispute was resolved and Dyson and Pinkerton were awarded £651-7s-0d for the work they had done, the balance being paid on 24 January 1792.

During the dispute James Smith continued working at the Stowmarket end and his contract with the Navigation Company was extended until 24 March 1792.

William Jessop's plan was to complete the canal in one year, but the first year of construction saw only a two mile stretch of river between Stowmarket and Needham Market completed, with just three locks of turf and timber.

RIVER GIPPING
TRUST

William Jessop was busy with several other contracts at the time the lawsuit settled in November 1791. The lack of progress led the Trustees to call upon John Rennie to resurvey the river in December 1791 and step in to complete the works.

Although all three of the original Jessop designed lock chambers remain, two have been rebuilt rather unsympathetically, but Badley Lock remains and it is thought to be one of the oldest turf and timber locks in the UK, though in rather desperate need of restoration.

Timber and turf-sided locks were common on river navigations during the 1700s as they were cheap and easy to build. Vertical walls, often made of brick, supported the lock gates and between the gates were sloping earth banks stabilised with grass and other plants. This design required a larger volume of water to fill the lock, slowing the transit of barges. Most were rebuilt with brick or stone, which required less maintenance, so that few remain in the UK.

# 4. John Rennie's survey, notes and map of the Gipping

John Rennie had surveyed several canals before the Gipping, although he had not led a canal construction. An inspection of the river was carried out in the presence of the Trustees on 13–15 December 1791. One week later he produced a report on 22 December 1791 that noted the section from Stowmarket to Needham Market was almost complete with three turf and timber locks, but that further locks and structures should be made of brick.

An initial four-page report was followed by 10 pages of estimates dated 16 April 1792.

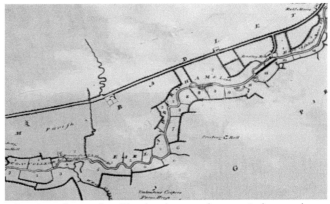

Section of map detailing landowners' property by number

Although the original plans supported the passing of an Act of Parliament, Rennie believed the first survey and detail of the works insufficient for the construction of the navigation. He was critical of Jessop's surveyor, Isaac Lenny, for his lack of accuracy and recommended a new survey.

Rennie wrote "The original Survey is very incorrect. I am surprised Mr Lenny should have paid so little attention to accuracy – this makes it necessary to set about a new Survey so as to lay down the true form of the River with the different works to be proposed. The Side Cuts should be laid down and the places of the Locks marked out. When this is completed the ground for the foundation of the Locks should be bored which will enable me to point out the proper mode of laying down the foundation of each". And that "in every work it is a wise maxim to lay down a proper plan on the first outset and to pursue the same with diligence afterwards. In this case the general outlines previous to obtaining the Act of Parliament seems to have been well pointed out by Mr Jessop but the proper steps to be pursued afterwards have been neglected. A regular Survey of the River should have been taken and the works to be executed properly laid down".

John Rennie produced a plan of the Proposed project for the Ipswich to Stowmarket Navigation in 1792. The plan showed every landowners' property area and its length of river frontage, essential to ensure no future legal disputes. It also clearly showed where new 'shorter' cuts were needed to make navigation possible and on whose property they lay.

*REFERENCE to Lands lying on West Side of the River Gipping* (handwritten tabular reference of Parishes, Proprietors, Length, and Occupiers — largely illegible)

He estimated the total additional costs to be £12,350 of which £6,600 would be needed for the remaining 12 locks at £550 each and recommended that another Act of Parliament should be obtained to raise more money. The Act was obtained on 28 March 1793, which authorised the Trustees to borrow an extra £15,000, as the original capital had all been spent. The final cost of construction was £26,263, nearly double the original estimate.

Rennie wrote that "In the future conduct of these works you must have some person who understands Brick making, Brick Locks and Bridges with the proper composition of Mortar. As for your present Resident Engineer, I doubt not is inadequate thereto and it will be very necessary that such a person should carry with him that kind of authority to ensure the execution of the works as directed for without authority there is no certainty of things being properly done. Such a person I shall endeavour, although I cannot absolutely promise, to find".

Rennie did indeed find such a person, and this person was Richard Coates. Coates was appointed surveyor at a salary of £200 p.a., as somebody with knowledge of bricklaying and masonry work.

Soon after Rennie had met with trustees he went on to make an agreement with Goodey, a brick maker in Ipswich early in 1792. So, we know for sure that Rennie was responsible for changing the lock design along the canal from turf and timber to brick. Rennie specifically stated that all road bridges over the river should be of brick construction.

The top plan illustrated below shows the current route of the river between Claydon and Needham Market, including the 'old river' in purple which starts at the large weir adjacent to Needham Lakes, this acts as a by-wash around Bosmere and Creeting locks. The old river was modified further when the railway line was built (it used to run the other side of the railway).

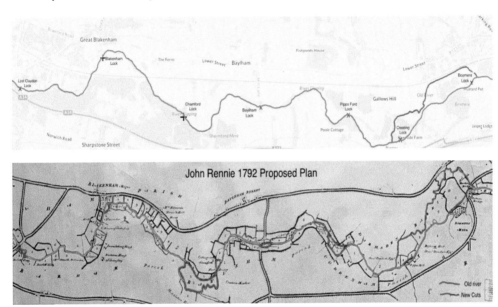

The lower John Rennie plan highlights his planned new cuts in red and the old river course in purple. Note, that not all of his planned new cuts were made.

The navigation was opened throughout on 14 September 1793. It was just under 16 miles (27 km) long from Ipswich to Stowmarket, rising 90 feet (27 m) through 15 locks of broad construction, each 55 by 14 feet (16.8 by 4.3 m). It was suitable for barges with a draught of 3 feet 4 inches (1.02 m).

John Rennie's 1792 Plan of the Ipswich to Stowmarket Navigation was on a scroll approximately ten feet long.

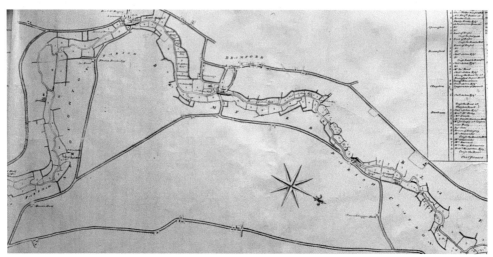

John Rennie's Ipswich to Blakenham Plan

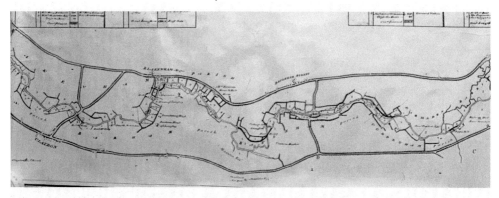

John Rennie's Claydon to Needham Market Plan

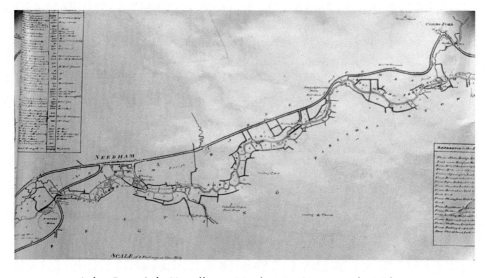

John Rennie's Needham Market to Stowmarket Plan

# 5. John Rennie and the importance of brickwork

Before John Rennie's involvement in canals, most river locks were made of turf and timber and many bridges were of timber. Rennie believed that canal locks and bridges should be made of brick. This required both bricks and mortar to be made to a higher specification to withstand permanent submersion in water.

In December 1791 he wrote that:

- "In the future conduct of these works you must have some person who understands Brick making, Brick Locks and Brick Bridges with the proper composition of Mortar.

- I would advise that the three timber locks now executed should stand, but the others to be done of Brick", and… "I shall send you a person to make the Survey above mentioned in February or March next and I shall allow for a few days myself to see matter put in a proper train".

- It would be absolutely necessary to find a resident engineer who understood brick making and brick building.

And he wrote that all future locks:

- To be done of Brick, plenty of which I doubt not will be found in the course of the proposed Navigation - at least if earth cannot be had of a sufficient good quality to make front Bricks it may be for those that are used in doing the Back or Inside parts of the Lock Walls and good ones may be furnished for the face. And that:

- Timber Locks from being exposed so frequently to Wet and Dry in the chamber and the Side next the ground being constantly damp soon decay and will in time injure much to the Navigation and Mills. And that:

- Given directions to search for bricks and I hope the rest of the Trustees will accordingly join them in preparing a sufficiency to proceed with expedition on the Locks and other works against next Spring.

In the 1790s, bricks were handmade in a wooden mould. Clay dug out of the ground in the winter months was left to break down. After the risk of frost had passed, water was added to the clay and the mix placed in brick moulds. These were left to dry in the open air for several weeks. The kilns used for firing had a range of temperatures inside, depending on the stacking method, so that bricks from the same kiln were not of a standard colour, or composition.

Creeting Bridge brickwork. Grade II listed
Photo taken by the author

The variability in the brick-work of this period is a visual delight which can mature with age.

Early in 1792, John Rennie came to an agreement with Goodey, a brick maker in Ipswich.

Each of the 12 locks required around 50,000 bricks. In total, the 12 locks and 20 bridges would have used about a million bricks.

A typical brickworks would make some 20,000-40,000 bricks a week, but it was seasonal work. Until the canal was built, these were transported by horse and cart to sites, which could account for around 50% of their cost. In later projects Rennie set up brick works adjacent to the canal to minimise transportation costs and this may have been the case along the Gipping.

Both of the Baylham and Bosmere bridges are built into the tail of the brick lock, to minimise the number of bricks used. As the towing horse didn't go through the lock, there was no need for a towpath under the bridge. Each bridge is of minimal width and height for a single barge to pass through.

# 6. John Rennie's Resident Engineer

After John Rennie had spent three days surveying the river, he submitted a report on 22 December 1791, stating that he would endeavour to find a resident engineer who understood brick making and brick building.

His choice was Richard Coates who was appointed as a surveyor on 1 March 1792 at a salary of £200 p.a. and went on to become the resident engineer. Coates was probably a mason with a good working knowledge of bricklaying and masonry. By the middle of April, when Rennie visited the works again, a bricklayer and a carpenter had arrived from the Basingstoke Canal to take charge of the structures.

In Rennie's 1792 notes to the Stowmarket Navigation Company, the detailed costs needed to complete the canal are attributed to Richard Coates' estimates. The ten-page estimate lists 100's of items, some less than £1. There is a single item of 12 locks at £6,600, which is probably a detailed estimate for one lock (£550) multiplied by 12. The costing by Coates would likely be based on a lock design drawing made by Rennie. This drawing would specify the length, width and average depth. It would specify lock gate size and lock chamber brick wall thickness, possibly including the number of bricks needed for its construction.

For the 20 bridges Rennie specified several designs. Coates costed these from £30 for a foot bridge to £300 for the bridge at Claydon. These costings indicate Coates had experience of contract work and contract estimates.

It was said that the previous Surveyor / Resident Engineer (James Smith) took on the employees of the sacked contractor workforce and carried on with canal construction before Rennie and Coates' involvement. This same arrangement could well have continued with Coates, more so when we know that John Hamer, the bricklayer and James Wilkins, the carpenter had arrived from the Basingstoke Canal to take charge of the structures, thus helping Coates.

As Principal or Consulting Engineer, it was Rennie's responsibility to find a suitable Resident Engineer. A variety of skills were required and suitable people with the requisite ability, integrity and experience were hard to find. The Resident Engineer was always employed by the client and Rennie made it clear that he would not be responsible for his nominee's conduct.

The Resident Engineers were authorised to improve Rennie's plans as they became more familiar with the nature and lay of the ground. They could determine the positions of bridges in consultation with landowners and Trustees. In later canal projects, Resident Engineers who departed from Rennie's plans without authority were dismissed.

Richard Coates left in October 1793 with a £50 gratuity and immediately set to work on the Chelmer and Blackwater Navigation in Essex, some 40 miles away. John Rennie had been appointed as their engineer and work began in July 1793 at the Chelmsford end with Coates acting as resident engineer, on £240 p.a. Coates took with him 50 men from the 200 Stowmarket workforce.

Richard Coates' brother George, a stonemason, continued working on the Ipswich to Stowmarket Navigation until 1798. He also worked with Richard on the construction of Chelmer and Blackwater Navigation.

Coates is not known for other civil engineering works, his correspondence with Rennie only covers the period 1793-1799. He went on to become a successful coal and timber merchant in Chelmsford who left £17,750 when he died in 1822.

Richard Coates is credited as the man who built the Chelmer and Blackwater Canal, but he should also receive credit for the Ipswich to Stowmarket Navigation. Once John Rennie had surveyed and engineered a proposed canal he rarely visited the site again. Most of the work was left to the resident engineer, with Rennie keeping in touch by mail.

When the Chelmer was completed it is believed Rennie offered Coates a post as resident engineer in other works. Instead he chose to settle at the head of the Chelmer and Blackwater Navigation to become a major barge owner and merchant. His name is remembered at Coates Quay in Springfield Basin, Chelmsford and he was buried in All Saints Church, a mile away.

Richard Coates Burial Chamber at Chelmsford. Photo taken by the author

On his death, his nephew, Brown, took over the business and he carried on trading with his son under the name of Brown & Son. Brown & Son developed into a large general builders' merchant and continued to bring its supplies of softwood up the navigation until 1972 when, on the take-over of the firm, the practice was discontinued and the small fleet of lighters disposed of. Travis Perkins still has a yard at the side of the navigation.

# 7. Building the Canal

The canalised sections of the Ipswich to Stowmarket Navigation were dug out by hand by men called Navigators, in later years shortened to Navvies. It is believed the workforce employed during its construction was around 200.

In the days before the Gipping was canalised, many of our Inland rivers were used to transport raw materials, such as coal, limestone and timber. These stretches of navigable rivers were known as navigations. The Gipping therefore was a navigation many years before it was canalised. Much engineering work was undertaken across the country to improve the navigability of these rivers when commercial canals began to be constructed in the 1750s.

Navvies used spades, picks and wheelbarrows to cut the channels. Horses were used to help with carrying and pulling. Once dug, a canal channel, or 'cut' was lined with 'puddle' (compressed wet clay) as a waterproof layer. The clay was packed hard by driving sheep and cattle down the canal.

Originally most navvies were local farm labourers, but by 1792, many navvies were travelling from one canal job to another. The navvies were the highest paid manual workers in the land, earning twice as much as a farm labourer. These navvies worked hard and lived hard. It took up to a year to turn a common labourer into a navvy capable of excavating 20 tons of earth per day.

"I've been a canal cutter upward of forty years," said John Walker in 1801, a professional navvy "I worked upon the Duke of Bridgewater's Canal" (1760s). Men who began there as labourers left it as Navigators, tramping away to spend the rest of their lives digging waterways across the country. It has been estimated that there were between five to ten thousand navvies working on Britains canals, many of whom overlapped into the railways in the 1820s. The civil engineering expertise in designing cuts, embankments, aqueducts and tunnels for canals was fundamental to the success of the railway mania that followed.

John Rennie is accredited with building many canals after the Ipswich to Stowmarket Navigation completion and he is admired for his revolutionary vision, but it is likely he never picked up a spade or laid a brick. It was the hardy navvies who dug the Canal and who went on to build the thousands of miles of waterway we enjoy today.

Many historians put the building of canals down to Contractors. By the 1790s there were a number of canal building contractors up and down the country. Many of these were major companies, from 1760 through to 1820 limited companies could only be set up by an Act of Parliament. They took on a range of canal work across the country at the same time. These contractors were responsible for the construction of specified lengths of waterways, including locks and bridges. They in turn would employ the workmen who would do the actual building. They recruited and employed the skilled craftsmen (carpenters, masons and bricklayers) and the large armies of labourers, the navvies.

This system suited the canal companies, who were spared the expense of purchasing all the equipment needed for construction, and all the bother of hiring men and paying wages. This system was initially used by the Stowmarket Navigation Company.

In April 1790, adverts appeared in the Oxford Journal (and other regional newspapers) with a request for experienced contractors to build 14 locks, some timber bridges, and widening, deepening and cutting of bends of the river between Stowmarket and Ipswich.

Three tenders were received and Contracts were awarded in July 1790 to George Pinkerton and John Dyson (who had already done much canal work across the country), but by October both had been dismissed. The already appointed Surveyor, James Smith took over, presumably employing the dismissed contractor's workforce and Samual Wright

> *Stowmarket Navigation, in the County of Suffolk.*
>
> ANY experienced Person or Persons, who may be willing to contract for the Building fourteen Locks of Brick, some Timber Bridges, and other Works, and for Widening, Deepening, Embanking, and Cutting off Bends of the River between Stowmarket and Ipswich, may see Designs and a Specification of the Work by applying to Mr. Norman of Stowmarket; and, after having, by a Survey of the River, &c. got the necessary Measurements and Information, they may deliver in their Proposals, sealed up, on or before the 24th Day of May next, to the said Mr. Norman, and the Work will be contracted for on the 7th Day of June, at the King's Head in Stowmarket.
> An experienced Workman, who can act in the Capacity of a Surveyor, and be well recommended, to engage under a Salary, to overlook the Execution of the Work, will receive due Encouragement.

of Ipswich was contracted to build six locks in a year from June 1791. By the end of 1791, three turf and timber locks had been built. John Rennie became involved in December 1791 and wanted to replace these with more durable and efficient brick locks (each estimated at £550, as they were all of the same design and construction).

There appears to be no further evidence of major contractor tendering after John Rennie and Richard Coates' involvement, so maybe Coates' estimates were used by the company as a project tracking document allowing him to project manage the work directly.

# 8. Barges along the Canal

Initially, there were up to four barges working on the navigation, which soon increased to 10. These barges were recorded as making over 30 trips/week in the early 1800s. The main cargo was manure which travelled toll free, coal, gun cotton, corn and hops. In the first full year of uninterrupted trade the total tolls received were £937.50 and the estimated expenses for that year were £380.

Footbridge and barges at Stowmarket Quay in 1838. RGT Historic Website Image

Enlarged text at the bottom of the etched drawing

It would appear that the canal was successful and profitable in the first 50 years, until the railway came along in 1846. The Evening Star in 1907 gave an account from a Stowmarket resident who worked as a barge assistant in 1843. He was quoted as saying that: "When the canal was in full working order" (up to the year 1850) "21 barges were running between Ipswich and Stowmarket. Messrs Thomas Prentice and Co owning 13" (a chemical company in Stowmarket later the gun cotton manufacturer) "they carried malt, wheat, barley and English corn to Ipswich bringing back coal, timber, salt and general goods".

"To enable the barges to turn, a 'basin' was constructed at the Pickerel Bridge at Stowmarket…. The barges were narrow in construction drawing three feet of water, and were manned by a captain, an assistant and a lad to see after the horses."

"The locks were filled and emptied by the bargemen themselves, and the journey occupied about nine hours if light, and twelve to thirteen if loaded. A full load consisted of about 400-450 sacks of malt, or 240 sacks of wheat, or 30 tons' coal."

"The time on the journey varied according to the depth of the water, numerous 'shoals' existing between Stowmarket and Baylham Mill, then known as Wicks Mill."

Horse pulling a barge, with Shrubland Hall in background. RGT Historic Website Image

"If a barge got caught by a 'shoal' a horse was put on a 'snatch block' and by the aid of a neighbouring tree, the barge was hauled over. Ten men were regularly employed in the district in keeping the waterway clear. Captains wages in those days were 12s per week, but he made a good addition by unloading and loading the cargo."

The Evening Star reported that although the Stowmarket resident had worked hard all his life, and was in his 76th year, he was still hale and hearty, and boasted that he had never smoked a pipe of tobacco in his life.

Titled 'Navigation Wharf Stowmarket". RGT Historic Website Image.

The barge in the image above is thought to be a Norfolk Wherry, sailed on the Norfolk and Suffolk Broads and rarely if ever sailed around the coast and unlikely to have sailed up the Gipping as the river is too narrow and has too many bridges to get under. An artist impression?

IMT Image Archive. Gipping Barge Mersey. Leonard Woolf Collection

The Evening Star in 1907, also reported that there was a movement to restore the canal between Stowmarket and Ipswich, as the canalised River Gipping was now only used for navigation purposes between Bramford and Ipswich. Above Bramford, it had become blocked following the expiration in 1887 of the lease with the railway company to maintain the navigation.

Commissioners Inspection on a Packard Barge. RGT Historic Website Image

IMT Image archive. Gipping barge Trent at Bramford lock c.1895. Harry Walters collection

When the railway arrived in 1846, the canal saw a large decline in water-borne trade. The Trustees sought Parliamentary approval to lease the navigation to the Eastern Union Railway for 42 years. In 1888 when the lease ended, the navigation was returned to the Trustees along with £2,000 compensation as it was in such a poor condition and then began the canal's demise between Bramford and Stowmarket. Travelling time along the waterway was then reported as being around ten hours going upstream and seven hours downstream and that in its heyday, there were up to 30 barges working carrying cargoes of coal, slates, timber, lime and manure. In later days chemicals and gun cotton were transported.

Initially all the boats were worked individually and were horse drawn. Steam barges frequented the lower part of the navigation around the turn of the century, operated by Packard's and Fisons. These barges towed one or two butties and they developed their own house style.

Fisons barges had white funnels, with names of Whale, Dragon and Scorpion being used. Packard's boats originally had black funnels but later changed to black and white. These barges were named after rivers, some recorded names are the Deben, Yare, Stour, and Trent River.

IMT Image Archive. Yare at Pin Mill. Stuart Grimwade Collection

The Yare was purchased by Suffolk Artist Jack Haste and moored at Pin Mill. She was sold in 2015 for use as a holiday home.

## Packards Barge Trent River

Captain George Glading (1864 – 1937) and married with 10 children was skipper of the Barge Trent River from 1916. It is reported that during his career, he saved the lives of 12 people by pulling them out of the river, the last one was when he was 58 years old, rescuing a lad from the Orwell, when he was fully clothed with boots on.

**SAVED TWELVE LIVES**

While passing through Messrs. William Brown and Sons' wharf yesterday Mr. George Glading, of 1, New Cut East, Ipswich, died suddenly.

Mr. Glading, who was 73 years of age, was a cheerful and friendly personality who was well-known in the Ipswich Dockland.

Since 1916 he had been skipper of the barge Trent River, which originally belonged

He received the Royal Humane Society bronze medal in 1902 for rescuing a 7 year old boy when he plunged in from his barge, swam 100 yds and brought the boy out.

When he retired in 1933 (after 53 years' service), he bought the Barge Trent River from his employer and continued to sail it. He claimed to be the only man living who had proceeded from Stowmarket to London by water.

to Messrs. Fison, Packard and Prentice Ipswich, by whom Mr. Glading was employed. When he retired in 1933, 53 years' service, the firm sold him barge, and he continued to sail it.

IMT Image Archive. Tug TRENT RIVER at Bramford

# 9. Industry along the Canal

In 1854, Edward Packard built a warehouse at the side of the Gipping at Bramford, he pioneered the production of artificial fertilisers for horticulture on an industrial scale. Packard was joined in 1858 by Joseph Fison who constructed his chemical works opposite.

IMT Image Archive. A Packard Barge on Bramford Quay. Harry Walters Collection

A lock was constructed, Bramford Lock with a quayside through a dock gate. The whole complex grew to become a busy industrial colossus, providing vital jobs in what was in effect a very isolated rural part of the county.

There was even an on-site pub, the White Elm that existed right up until 1974.

The factory closed in 2003 and was Grade II listed, it was burnt down in 2019.

The Factory on Fire – 2019. Courtesy SkyCamEast

Not far from Blakenham Lock on the other side of the lakes, at the end of a road called Pesthouse Lane, there once stood an old workhouse with an interesting history and a little bit of folklore. This House of Industry was built in 1765 and demolished in 1963. In 1850, inmates rioted and again in 1851 causing more damage and ransacking the institution's kitchens. The desperate men who rioted were starving, claiming their meagre rations never quelled their hunger. It is said that a visitor back in the early days was none other than Charles Dickens, researching social conditions of the time and it is said that here he found the inspiration for his famous novel Oliver Twist. During WW2 the 'House of Industry' housed Italian prisoners-of-war.

Manganese Bronze set up a foundry during WW1 at the site of the former Handford Hall Farm. They manufactured artillery shell cases and later bearings, including the bearings that support Sydney Harbour Bridge.

Stowmarket prospered after the navigation opened. Within a few years the population had doubled and industries were springing up by the river. Many of today's main industries in Stowmarket owe their origins to the navigation and retain their riverside sites.

One of its first industries was malt for brewing. From the late eighteenth through to the early twentieth century, Stowmarket was second only to Burton-on-Trent for its malt product output. At its height, the town had seventeen maltings, most of them along the river bank.

Gun cotton was discovered in 1846, it is also known as nitrocellulose. A highly explosive cellulose nitrate, made by digesting clean cotton in a mixture of one part nitric acid and three parts sulphuric acid. It replaced gunpowder as a propellant in firearms. Thomas Prentice & Company began manufacturing gun cotton in Stowmarket in 1863 at a newly built factory on the banks of the river. The Prentice family was prominent in Stowmarket at the time and operated a number of other businesses including a gas works, corn and coal merchants. An explosion in the gun cotton works in 1871 claimed 28 lives and left 75 injured with wide spread destruction. After the explosion, the factory was rebuilt in 1872 and the new company operated as the Stowmarket Guncotton Company.

During the first world war the factory made Stowmarket a target. On 31 March 1916, it was the intended destination of the German Zeppelin L13; it was hit with anti-aircraft fire prior to reaching the town. The factory merged to form part of the Imperial Chemical Industries (ICI) and makes paint. One of the country's main ICI - Dulux paint plants evolved from Prentice's Chemical and Explosives works.

Ruins of Gun-cotton works at Stowmarket. RGT Historic Website Image

In 1914, a young man called Louis Tibbenham took on part of a factory in Stowmarket which had gone bankrupt, and set up his own company, the Suffolk Iron Foundry, to make castings such as flywheels and ploughshares. In 1925 the company added lawn mowers to their range of products. They then introduced the Suffolk Punch cylinder lawn mower in 1954.

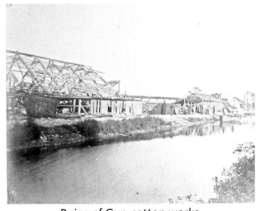

Ruins of Gun-cotton works.
RGT Historic Website Image

'PUNCH' with Dual Drive ★

14 CUT

4-STROKE
EASY-START
POWER UNIT

36½ GNS

THE SUFFOLK 'PUNCH' STANDARD MODEL
STILL COSTS ONLY 36 GNS INCLUDING GRASS BOX Tax Paid

Www.oldlawnmowerclub.Co.uk

Many thousands of Suffolk Punch cylinder machines were sold in the UK and overseas making it an incredibly popular machine. They were the most reliable domestic motor mowers ever to be produced in the UK and still to this day have a very loyal band of dedicated followers.

Suffolk Punch became part of the Atco Qualcast group. The Stowmarket site is now home to research and development in the UK for Bosch Power Tools home and garden products.

# 10. Some Original Bridges along the Canal

Most, but not all, of the original 1793 bridges built to cross the new navigation have long since disappeared but some photos remain.

Luckily, (for history records) a legal dispute arose between 1890 and 1897 over the liabilities for repair of several of the bridges. The council wanted the responsible owners (the trustees of the navigation) to repair Sproughton, Bramford Bridge and others.

It was referred to arbitration using these photos as evidence of similarly styled bridges, all built one hundred years earlier by the navigation company.

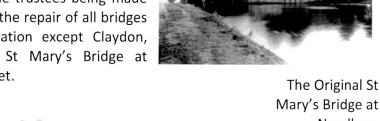

The original Stowupland, Bramford and Sproughton Bridges. 1890s photos

It resulted in the trustees being made responsible for the repair of all bridges over the navigation except Claydon, Handford and St Mary's Bridge at Needham Market.

The Original St Mary's Bridge at Needham Market was replaced by a concrete bridge in 1922 using the original 1793 brick abutments.

From Suffolk Archaeology. https://suffolkarchaeology.co.uk/reports-pdfs/2008_120.pdf

John Rennie's 1792 notes detail a list of bridges required for the Navigation together with their estimated costs.

| | |
|---|---|
| Handford Bridge | £150 |
| Bridge at tail of first lock | £40 |
| Bridge opposite to Chantry | £102 |
| Bridges at Sproughton and Bramford | £300 |
| A Swing bridge called Bishops Bridge | £70 |
| Bridge at Paper Mill | £120 |
| Footbridge called Old Mill Bridge | £30 |
| Claydon Bridge at tail of lock | £40 |
| Bridge at Blakenham Mill | £150 |
| Supposed bridge in Msrs Edwards Land | £102 |
| In new cut by Shamford Hall | £40 |
| Foot bridge by Shamford Hall | £30 |
| Baylham Mill lock tail | £50 |
| Road Bridge Poolhouse Farm, Baylham | £102 |
| Road Bridge by Pipps Farm, Pipps Ford | £102 |
| Bridge at Tail of Creeting Lock | £40 |
| Bridge at Bosmere Mill | £142 |
| Bridges at Needham will cost to finish | £40 |

Above: Pickerel Bridge, Stowmarket.

Above right: Footbridge over the river at Crown Street, Needham Market

Right: Claydon Bridge 1890

RGT Historic Website Images

Sproughton Bridge.
Both photos, RGT website. John Jarman Postcard collection

# Bramford Bridge

The old timber bridge at Bramford, which was thought to be the original, was replaced in 1904.

But in January 1939 East Anglia had some of the worst floods for over a century and the new bridge was swept away.

The Original Ship Lane Bridge, Bramford 1903
RGT Website. John Jarman Postcard Collection

The new 1904 Bridge that was washed away
RGT Website. John Jarman Postcard Collection

A resident of Baylham told the Trust that she was among a bunch of school children being ferried home by a local farmer in his horse and cart but just as the last load came up to the bridge, the horse refused to move another inch.

Seconds later the bridge was washed away.

A 'temporary' Bailey bridge was installed but it took another 10 years for a proper bridge to be erected.

Ship Lane Bridge Bramford 1939.
RGT Historic Website Image

# 11. Water Mills along the Gipping

Once, there were around twelve mills operating along the Gipping. Here are some known details of the mills from Stowmarket to Ipswich:

### Hawks Mill, Needham Market

The present mill was constructed in 1884 and a date stone is incorporated into the front of the four-storey red-brick building. It was extended in 1892 with the addition of two wings, each two storeys tall plus attics. It has a pantiled roof and a white-painted weather boarded lucam.

Hawks Mill around 1884. RGT Historic Website Image

The original Mill was part of the manor of Creeting endowed by Henry VI to Eton College in 1441. The lease in 1542 refers to "the haute mylle' which in French means high or upper mill. This was to differentiate it from the lower mill at Bosmere which at the time was also owned by Eton College.

In 1623, a clerk issued a new lease but misread the original words and wrote it as 'hauke mill'. By 1683 it had become Hawks Mill. There is no evidence of anyone named Hawk ever leasing the mill. Mills on this site have been used to produce flour, paper and even mustard when it was owned by Reckitt & Colman during the 2nd World War.

In its working days, the 1884 Hawks Mill was a traditional corn mill but used an Armfield water turbine in lieu of a waterwheel. This was said to still be in place and capable of operating in the early 1980s, although the milling machinery had already been taken out.

Hawks Mill around 1870. RGT Historic Website Image

It is now converted to residential flats, but retains much of its character and charm. Hawks Mill is in a picturesque loc-ation on the River Gipping above a late eighteenth-century bridge.

Grade II listed.

Mill and Bridge. His-toric England listing no. 1277199.

Hawks Mill. Photo taken by the author

https://historicengland.org.uk/listing/the-list/list-entry/1277199?section=official-listing

## Bosmere (Barking) Mill, Needham Market

Converted to residential use but retaining much of its character and charm, it is located adjacent to Bosmere Lock and the popular Needham Lake and Nature Reserve.

Bosmere Mill was built in the late eighteenth or early nineteenth century and is four storeys tall plus an attic. In contrast to Hawks Mill it is timber framed and the weatherboarding is painted black. It has a concrete tiled roof, half-hipped at the north end. A gabled Lucam (hoist loft) projects from the east roof slope.

Bosmere Mill, Cart Lodge and Lock
RGT Website. John Jarman Postcard Collection

Bosmere Mill and lock. Photo taken by the author

The Grade II-listed building was once used as a restaurant, it is now converted into flats. A large iron breast-shot water-wheel remains, which was formerly in a wheelhouse but is now external.

All milling machinery has been removed.

Formerly known as Barking Road Mill or Quinton's Mill, marked on Hodskinson's 1783 map (S1) and on Kirby's map of 1736 (S3). Historic England Listing no 1231764

https://historicengland.org.uk/listing/the-list/list-entry/1231764?section=official-listing

## Creeting Mill (also referred to as Bosmere Lower Mill)

The former Bosmere / Creeting Mill, adjacent to Creeting lock, stood about 800m down river from Bosmere / Barking Mill.

Creeting Mill. RGT Website. John Jarman Postcard Collection

The last lock keeper was Samuel Ward who lived (in 1927) with his 33 year old wife, his 83 year old mother and his 8 year old daughter. Les Ward was a later edition to the family born in 1930.

Samuel was not strictly a 'lock keeper' as by this time he was blind and unable to work.

The last residents of Creeting Mill (1932)
RGT Historic Website Image

As a result of his blindness, he and his family had been evicted from their previous home in a tied cottage belonging to Pipps Farm. At this time the Mill was owned by the Saumarez family of Shrubland Hall and they allowed Samuel and his family to live in the cottage attached to the mill.

Les can remember leading his father to the lock to operate the paddles on the top gates but this was to control water flow further downstream.

The bottom gates were always left open and in any case by this time (1934-35) there were no boats passing through the lock at all.

Florence, Les and Elsie Ward. RGT Historic Website Image

The cottage was flooded out in 1936 and the family moved to Needham Market. Samuel died in 1959.

Just before the First World War, a German spy, 'The Baron', was living in the cottage at the rear of Bosmere Mill and he quite often booked a first class passage from Stowmarket to Germany and returned via Parkeston Quay.

Adrien Pryke was a Telegraph Messenger in Needham Market living with his grandmother in Back Lane. One day just after war broke out he was asked to deliver a telegram to the Baron. Whilst telegram boy Pryke was at the front door, hordes of Special Branch men crashed in through the back door and caught the villain in the hen run.

Adrien was congratulated by the security team and they gave him the lamp from the Baron's bike as a keepsake. Adrien eventually died in Needham at the age of 97 in 1994.

The Mill was demolished in the mid-twentieth century.

## Baylham Watermill and Mill House

The only complete watermill on the River Gipping, and is Grade II listed. The mill is of early or mid-19th century, 3 storeys, with storage bins in the 4th attic storey. The ground storey is of red brick, which is now painted. Timber-framed upper storeys are weatherboarded with plain tiled roofs. A two-storey, gabled, weatherboarded hoist is cantilevered on diagonal braces.

Baylham Mill and bridge around 1900. RGT Website. John Jarman Postcard collection

The mill was still being used to grind corn in the early 1960s. The last miller was Jubilee Montague Chambers who was born in Baylham in 1887 and died in 1969. The then owner's son can remember Jubilee sitting on the bridge parapet with a large knife with which he used to carve his lunchtime bread and cheese.

In the 1960s there was a bounty paid for the number of rats that you could kill. To prove the number, you had to produce the rat's tail, so Jubilee would have used the same knife for both his lunch and cutting the rats' tails.

The main machinery consists of a cast iron breast-shoe waterwheel on an iron shaft, driving a wooden lineshaft via an all-iron pitwheel and pinion. Three pairs of millstones on a hurst frame are driven via 3 wooden compass-arm gearwheels mounted on the lineshaft (2 now incomplete). Two further pairs of stones could be driven by water or by the auxiliary oil engine (by E.R. & F. Turner of Ipswich).

All 5 pairs of stones are complete with their furniture and much ancillary machinery. The house is in two sections, early 16th century or earlier and mid nineteenth century.

This building and surrounding land was part of the Shrubland Estate which was put up for sale in September 1941. The mill and land were purchased by Ernest Norman Onians using the money he made from selling 'Tottenham Pudding' - pig swill from waste food, made from leftovers collected from the back door of London restaurants which earned himself the nickname of 'The Pudding King', all said to have been processed at Baylham Mill.

Above Baylham Mill and Lock. RGT Historic Website Image

During the 1940s and 1950s he started buying objects at country house sales and stashed them away in the mill and outbuildings. After his wife Daphne (a former model) died in 1983 he became a virtual recluse surrounded by hundreds of paintings, furniture, clocks and china ware. The locals thought it was junk, as did the people who carried out three robberies at his home over the years but only took some cash.

An employee's wife working for Ernest Onians in the 1980s wrote that…. "What made him rich, see, was his own shrewd ways. After the First War every-body with a pig in their back garden needed some way of feeding it. What was wanting was proper feed. So, he sees his chance and starts collecting all the food scraps he can get. Can't say as how he went from point A to point B, but next thing you know he's got loads of food coming up the River Gipping on barges what he already has connections with and it all comes out to him at old Baylham Mill.

In the three or four years I was there, we got most of the mill working and the exterior painted. He (Ernest) wanted me to work on the water-wheel but we never got around to it. You couldn't test some parts without water. See, in the '60s there was some change to the waterways. I don't know much about it, except the lock gates were broken on the River Gipping and nobody would pay for their repair. Therefore, Baylham Mill and all the others are broken down for good."

Over a period of 40 years, until his death in 1994, Ernest Onians amassed a sprawling art collection of over 1,000 items including 500 canvases, described as the the art find of the decade by the Ipswich Star. One of those items was a painting bought for £12 in the 1940s. When authenticated some 50 years later as a lost Poussin masterpiece, some art experts valued it at £12 million.

The painting was discovered under a sack of other paintings in a shed, that is now quite possibly the River Gipping Trust's wooden site hut. Sotheby's valued it at £15,000, but it sold for £155,000. After it was cleaned and restored, experts at the Louvre gallery in Paris confirmed it as a 1626 Poussin which disappeared some 350 years earlier.

A more recent photo of Baylham Mill.
Photo taken by the author

The Rothschild Foundation bought the masterpiece, 'The Destruction and Sack of Jerusalem' in 1998 for £4.5 million (said to be an eyewitness account of the Roman devastation of Jerusalem in AD70). Executors for the Onians sought compensation and sued Sotheby's for £4.5m, with an out of court settlement said to be a six-figure sum paid by Sotheby's a few years later.

The exterior of the Mill has been restored over the past few years, hopefully sometime in the future it will be fully restored and open to the public.

Water Mill and Mill House. Historic England Listing no. 1033260
https://historicengland.org.uk/listing/the-list/list-entry/1033260?section=official-listing

## Blakenham Mill

The mill was burnt down in 1928.

IMT Image Archive. Blakenham Mill c.1890. David Kindred Collection

Blakenham Mill 1928. RGT Historic Website Image

## Paper Mill, Bramford

Post- medieval water mill, brick and weather boarded with a slate roof. It was built as a paper mill and later converted to grind corn. The internal, breast-shot, iron water wheel survives. It is now converted to flats and offices. A watermill on this site is indicated on Hodskinson's map of 1783.

Old Paper Mill 1930. Courtesy The Mills Archive Trust

Now converted to flats and offices. Paper Mill lock can be seen on the left.
Photo taken by the author

## Bramford Mill

The Mill was built around 1860 and was one of the largest on the river with 11 pairs of stones. It was a working mill until an employee left a lighted hurricane lamp on a reciprocating sieve which fell to the floor and destroyed the weather boarded upper floors of the Mill in 1917.

Both the nearby Packards Works' steam fire engine and the never used before Bramford Fire Brigade's engine were on the scene when after around two hours of the fire starting, the roof, upper floors and heavy machinery fell through with a crash, accompanied by a huge upwards burst of fire and sparks. With the combined

Bramford Mill before the fire.
RGT Historic Website Image

efforts of both fire engines, they concentrated their efforts and saved the two houses close by.

The Mill owner (Mr William Cooper) received a bill of over £15 for costs incurred by the fire brigade, over half the original cost of the appliance, purchased in 1914 for £28-12s-6d. An employee of the Mill, working there around the time of the fire for 11 hours per day, earned around 10s (£0.50p) per week.

Bramford Mill after the fire.
RGT Historic Website Image

At the time of the fire, it was full of grain, a huge loss to the local community during the World War One famine times. A Water mill symbol is shown on Hodskinson's 1783 and Bowen's 1755 maps.

The Mill had a 12 hp compound beam engine by Wentworth of Wandsworth in 1888 and an 80 hp compound beam engine in 1908. A 1917 newspaper article tells more of the story.
https://www.bramfordhistorygroup.org.uk/100-years-ago-march-1917-a-newspaper-article-from-the-east-anglian-daily-times-of-friday-16th-march-1917/

## Sproughton Mill

Converted to residential use and retaining much of its character and charm, Sproughton Mill is a Grade II listed building and a typical example of an early industrial structure, probably dating to the 18th century. Two arches span the mill race beneath the building providing power to an undershot mill wheel, which is now removed.

Sproughton Mill around 1915.
RGT Website. John Jarman Postcard collection

The structure retains a high quality and picturesque brick façade and weatherboarded hoist loft extending from its upper floor. Massive Baltic softwood joists support several floors. The ground floor retains a robust oak frame, which formally enclosed the milling machinery, most of which is now removed.

Sproughton Mill. Photo taken by the author

This is Sproughton Mill with a wonderful Mill pond in the foreground. The mill itself dates from about 1820, being rebuilt by accomplished civil engineer Sir William Cubitt. William was Chief Engineer at Ransomes, the World-famous Ipswich engineering company, but he also worked on canals, docks and railways, as well as being the inventor of the old prison treadwheel.

There is evidence of previous mills on the same site:
- 1329 a Mill with 3 acres of land recorded
- 1747 old water mill recorded on the same spot as present day mill
- 1818 old mill demolished

The last miller at Sproughton Mill is thought to be Ernest Edwin Jacob from 1922 to 1946. Grade II listed English Heritage no 1036927
https://historicengland.org.uk/listing/the-list/list-entry/1036927

## Handford Water Mill, Ipswich

Handford Mill was a historic water mill located in Ipswich. The first record of the mill dates from 1323. In the nineteenth century, the mill was owned by Ipswich Corporation. In 1830 they leased it to Ezra Dalton. By 1840, this lease had been taken over by Samuel Webber who converted it into an oil mill.

IMT Image Archive. Handford Mill c.1848. Nick Wiggin Collection

This is Handford Mill, viewed across the millpond just downstream of today's Alderman Canal, formerly the River Little Gipping. This river is thought to be a man-dug water-way to power the water mill.

After the mill was demolished, the river was blocked off by the Victorians in the 1800s leaving just the millstream which we know today as the Alderman Canal, whilst the remainder was filled in and piped and is now used as a surface drainage duct entering the River Orwell just above Stoke Bridge. It is no longer a flowing river.

The water mill stood where flats now stand on the corner of Handford Road and Alderman Walk. Little Gipping Street, Friars Bridge Road and the "Wolsey Street Hump" where the river passed under the road near the former Zulu Inn, are all remnants and reminders of this former waterway.

# 12. The Gipping and the oldest photo in Suffolk
With grateful contributions from the Ipswich Maritime Trust, Stuart Grimwade and David Kindred

One of the earliest photos ever taken in Suffolk is of a Riverside Cottage at Sproughton. Quite possibly the then lock keeper's cottage.

The image above was made directly by David Kindred from the original John Wiggin wax paper negative of c1848. Some of his original negatives were 3 feet by 2 feet in size but most were 15 inches by 11 inches, giving prints of the same size. The National Photography Museum at Lacock has identified it as one of the most important surviving images in the history of photography. The detail is so good that an enlarged cropped image of the cottage and river bank can be clearly seen.

John Wiggin was an Ipswich pharmacist who became a pioneer of the then relatively new science of photography. He ran a chemist shop in Ipswich and became fascinated by the chemical processes that enabled scenes to be captured and preserved. He created dozens of images of Suffolk, of which the one of the riverside cottage and church at Sproughton survives, it is believed to have been taken in 1848.

Photographic portrait of John Wiggin (9-9-1818 to 7.1.1879) Courtesy
www.ipswich-lettering.co.uk/wigginchemist.html

The oldest known Gipping barge photo. IMT Image Archive. Robert Burrows Collection

Another of his surviving negatives is that of a barge on the Gipping at Sproughton, also dated 1848, maybe taken on the same day that he took the Riverside Cottage photo with all his large, heavy and cumbersome photographic equipment; no mean thing to do in the 1840s with only horse drawn vehicles and poor roads. It is possible that this barge photo was actually taken by his colleague and fellow pioneering photographer, Robert Burrows. Burrows liked to appear in his own images in his stove pipe hat and there is a figure like him sitting on the towpath bank. It is believed that Wiggin quite likely had to make his own camera as none were available to purchase at the time.

The earliest surviving negative image in the world was taken in 1835 by William Henry Fox Talbot when photography as we know it was born. Fox Talbot's creation was called the calotype and the process was patented in 1841. Essentially, it's this technique that John Wiggin embraced soon after Fox's discovery, it's quite likely that Wiggin was one of only around 50 people in the whole country who were involved in photography in 1848.

In 1855 at the London Photographic Society, he exhibited a photo of "Baylham Hall Suffolk, a Residence of Anne Boleyn on waxed-paper (cat no. 609)" and a year later two exhibits, one near Ipswich the other at Peterborough.

Wiggin's trade stand at an Ipswich Camera Club exhibition in November 1904;
Courtesy www.ipswich-lettering.co.uk/wigginchemist.html

John Wiggin's time as a Suffolk pioneer was important but quite short. By 1859, amateur photography in Britain had taken off in quite a big way with photographic magazines being published like 'Photographic News' that reported on "The means of recovering silver from its waste solutions", and of a photo taken that "was exposed for 9 minutes in bright sunshine". Clearly while today's camera magazines talk about megapixels or lens quality, the focus of the articles then was a bit different. Photographers of this time had to work directly with the chemical and natural elements at hand to produce anything at all.

Wiggin & Son's chemist's shop was on the corner of Berners Street and St Matthews Street. It sold pharmaceuticals, cosmetics, photographic equipment, lantern slide equipment, chemistry sets and other products.

The chemist shop remained in the Wiggin family until 1999 with Boots later taking it over and closing it in 2017.
https://www.ipswich-lettering.co.uk/wigginchemist.html

1840s photo of Wiggin's Chemist. Courtesy www.ipswich-lettering.co.uk/wigginchemist.html

IMT Image Archive. David Kindred Collection

This remarkable John Wiggin photo was taken around 1890. Originally thought to be Bramford's Ship Lane Bridge with Bramford Mill and Bramford lock in the distance. This photo is most probably not of the Gipping but Dedham on the Stour, taken as part of a set of the Stour Navigation.

This bridge photo differs slightly from other 'Ship Lane bridge' photos taken around the same time. This photo clearly has two sets of three support columns in the river. Other Bramford bridges of the 1900s era have four sets of four support columns. The mill also has a different number of windows across its width.

The 1890 - 1897 legal dispute over the liabilities for repair of Bramford and other bridges (chapter 10 refers) includes a photograph of the 'original' Bramford bridge with four sets of four support bridge columns.

# 13. Some old Navigational Newspaper articles

The Trust has searched through the British Newspaper Archive for any references to the Gipping and The Navigation over the past 230 years. Below are some of the articles found. Many more including a comprehensive index and links to the actual cutting (over 50) can be found on the Trust's website.

23 September 1789 - Bury and Norfolk Post were the first local newspaper to report that the Ipswich to Stowmarket Navigation was being promoted, at the same time as a navigation from Bury St Edmunds to Ipswich.

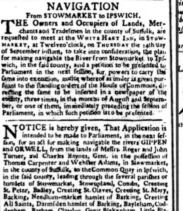

24 April 1790 - Oxford Journal - A request for contractors to build 14 locks, some timber bridges and widening, deepening and cutting of bends of the river.

20 August 1791 - Ipswich Journal - the sacked contractors were taking the Navigational Trustees to Court with the judge suggesting an independent valuer be appointed to assess how much they should be paid for the work done before they were dismissed.

3 August 1793 - Ipswich Journal - Navigation expected to open within a fortnight.

14 September 1793 - Ipswich Journal - Navigation Opens for Business.

14 February 1794 - Ipswich Journal - Report of damage to the Navigation by flooding. It was closed for repairs.

23 March 1805 - The Ipswich Journal reported that a 44-ton barge named Industry and a chestnut horse were up for auction along with 2 other barges, all at the head of Navigation in Stowmarket.

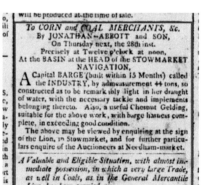

11 October - 1806 - The Commissioners of the Navigation increase the tolls by 25%!

26 September 1817 - Suffolk Chronicle - application is being made to Parliament for a navigable cut from Earl Stonham to join the River Gippen at Creeting All Saints.

19 September 1818 - The Ipswich Journal reported that an application is being made to Parliament for a navigable cut from Diss to join the river at Creeting All Saints.

2 January 1819 - Ipswich Journal – A meeting will be held at the White Lion Inn, Eye to take the report and estimates for the navigation between Diss and Ipswich.

11 January 1834 - Ipswich Journal reported that meetings were still being held about a Navigation from Earl Stonham to Needham Market. Mr Cubitt producing an estimate of £15,000.

> for this county.
> NAVIGATION FROM EARL STONHAM TO NEEDHAM MARKET.—A meeting of Owners and Occupiers of land in the Stonhams, and their vicinity, was held yesterday, (Friday), at the Pie Inn, Little Stonham, "for the purpose of adopting such measures as might be considered most desirable in order to render navigable a certain water course or river from the Turnpike Road at Stonham, to branch in with the Stowmarket Navigation at Needham." There were present J. E. Rust, Esq., the Rev.

1 March 1834 - Ipswich Journal - More talk about the Stonham Navigation. A new estimate of £8,000 was submitted "founded on the knowledge of practical men, and calculated on a liberal scale."

14 November 1835 - Ipswich Journal - reported that the good folks of Stonham propose to go to Parliament to bring in a bill to obtain an Act.

11 December 1841 - Ipswich Journal - The Commissioners of the Navigation and the barge masters were of the opinion that a second lock should be constructed in the New Dock.

15 January 1842 - Bells Weekly Messenger reported that the captain of the newly built in Ipswich sailing barge "Ironsides", which was used for carrying ale from Stowmarket to London, had fallen overboard and was crushed near a lock on the Gipping, and that a month later, his son was knocked overboard by the boom and lost after a strong gust of wind (in the Thames) and that later, the third hand fell overboard and also drowned.

> A few weeks since a new iron sailing barge was built in Ipswich, and named the Ironsides, for the conveyance of ale between Messrs. Stevens and Co.'s brewery, at Stowmarket, and their stores in Thames-street, London. On the return of the vessel from her first trip to London with Suffolk ale, while passing through a lock in the River Gippin, near Stowmarket, Baker, the captain of her, in easing her off from the side of the lock, fell overboard, while the horses on the towing-path were drawing her along, and he was so dreadfully crushed between the vessel and the jetty, that he died eight hours afterwards. Last week a young man named Baker, the son of the late captain, and mate of the same vessel, lost his life in the Swin during the night. The Ironsides was on her way from London to Stowmarket, laden with iron, &c., when a sudden gust of wind caught the sail, and the boom struck Baker a violent blow on the back, and, owing to the want of bulwarks on deck, he was forced overboard. The captain immediately lowered the sail,

10 July 1847 - The Suffolk Chronical reported that the Sailing Barge "GIPPING" was being sold at auction. She was 52ft 9ins by 13ft 9in and could carry 34 tons, and had been constantly employed in conveying goods between Stowmarket and London.

28 May 1864 - Ipswich Journal reported on the first serious explosion in Prentice's Gun Cotton Factory at Stowmarket. One girl, Fanny Burrows was killed and three others badly burned. Cobb, the foreman was saved from extensive facial injuries through the thickness of his beard! The inquest jury determined that there was insufficient evidence to determine the precise cause of the explosion.

21 April 1866 - Ipswich Journal has a detailed article about Prentice's Gun Cotton Works, Fisons Chemical Manure Works and the Stowmarket Paper Making Company.

5 February 1870 - Ipswich Journal - A bargeman, was accidentally drowned in the Gipping near the bridge leading to the station. This bridge was of timber construction and was probably the original bridge built when the station was in Croft Street. A platform had been constructed around the bridge piles to allow the man in charge of the horse to unhitch it before he walked round the platform and re-hitched the horse. The rails on this platform were broken and it was thought the Bargeman had slipped and fallen.

> **DEATH BY DROWNING NEAR IPSWICH RAILWAY STATION.**
>
> An inquest was held at the Station Hotel, Ipswich, on Thursday afternoon, before S. B. Jackaman, Esq., borough coroner, on the body of a bargeman, named Edward Abbott, who was accidentally drowned in the Gipping, near the bridge leading to the station, early that morning. The Gipping is at this point a tidal river, as the bridge is about half-a-mile below the last lock. The bridge is of timber, and as the upright piles supporting it are in the water-way, it is necessary to have a platform running from the towing path round the timbers, so as to enable the horsemen to carry the rope past the bridge. This platform is protected by a rail; but it appears that the rail is defective in places, and as the platform is very narrow, the unfortunate man appears to have fallen into the water, and he was drowned, as help could not be rendered by his companion in the darkness of the night. The body was not recovered till more than an hour afterwards, although every means was used by Mr. Henry Briggs, who was as usual, at that time, in charge of the Railway Station. There was some complaint concerning the condition of the bridge; and the Foreman, after the Jury had been sworn, expressed a wish on the part of the Jury to see the spot. The Coroner, however, recommended the Jury to wait till they had heard the evidence, and the first witness called was
>
> David Pinner, who said he was the captain of Mr. Fison's barge Scorpion. The barge, he said, plyed between Ipswich and Mr. Fison's manure manufactory situate at Bramford. The deceased man's name was Edward Abbott, and he was horse driver to the barge, and in the employ of Mr. Cole, carter, St. Peter's. Witness had known the deceased for more than 12 months, and three weeks ago he began working with the barge. He and the deceased

8 April 1876 - East Anglian Daily Times reported on the Great Fire of Bramford that destroyed Mr Godard's Tar Works and put in danger the factories of Packard and Fisons.

18 October 1884 - The Ipswich Journal reported that the annual inspection of the river between Stowmarket and Ipswich took place.

February to April 1889 - many newspaper articles reported on the proposal of a new Act to create a new navigation company which would abandon the navigation above Bramford. It was rejected.

2 May 1896 - Ipswich Journal reported on an Arbitration hearing between the county council and the navigation company over the responsibilities for repair of bridges crossing the river.

3 May 1906 - The Evening Star reported that £2,000 would be enough to make the Navigation between Bramford and Stowmarket fully navigable again.

2 September 1907 - The Evening Star reported that the Commissioners of the Navigation made their annual inspection on a steam barge provided by Packard and Co.

7 September 1909 - The Evening Star reported on the annual inspection of the Navigation being made from Gun Cotton Locks. The condition of the lock gates was such that they could not be used and it was agreed they should be repaired. They also noted a problem with pollution.

26 July 1941 - Bury Free Press - A major part of the Shrubland Estate was put up for sale, including Baylham Hall, Baylham House (now the Rare Breeds Farm) and Baylham Mill.

> The Baylham and Darmsden portions of
>
> ## THE SHRUBLAND ESTATE
> ### of 2,570 Acres,
>
> Comprising Baylham Hall and Tarston Hall Farms with period houses and moated Homesteads; Seven other farms; Baylham House; Baylham Mill; Baylham Fish Pond of 9 acres.
>
> Numerous Cottages in the Villages of Baylham, Darmsden and Great Blakenham. Long frontages to the main Norwich and Stowmarket Roads.

27 May 1949 - The Bury Free Press reported that Needham Market Parish Council had sent a telegram to Mr Attlee. "We appeal in desperation to the Prime Minister to stop the intolerable pollution of the River Gipping which has poisoned the life of the town for a quarter of a century."

3 February 2002 - Ipswich Star - Baylham Mill art collection and Sotheby's six figure compensation pay out.

21 August 2021 - Ipswich Star - Damaged Footbridge finally set to be repaired after nearly 80 years.

# 14. The Demise of the Navigation

In 1846, the Ipswich to Bury St Edmunds railway line was built. Much of the track followed the line of the river. The Stowmarket Navigation company decided to lease the canal to the railway company for a period of 42 years.

The railway company neglected the canal and undercut its tolls. When the lease expired in 1888 it refused to renew. By that time the upper part was in a poor state with little remaining traffic, with the last barges travelling to the explosive factory at Stowmarket around 1910.

In 1906, the Ipswich Evening Star reported that; "The canal, as every Ipswichian knows, is already in navigable condition as far as Bramford; and it is estimated that £2,000 would be sufficient to render the stretch between Bramford and Stowmarket serviceable for barges".

IPSWICH, THURSDAY, MAY 3, 1906.

To a large number of people it may come rather as a surprise that the Gipping, which is very generally looked upon as a natural river, is a canal within the meaning of the Act; not a canal in that it was dug out deliberately like a small edition of Suez, but that the bed and banks of a natural stream were so treated as to bring it under the heading of artificial waters. The "Gipping Canal" has a Conservancy Board, under the style of the Trustees of the Ipswich and Stowmarket Navigation, and this body are considering the question of the possibility of the canal coming within the scope of the Royal Commission appointed to deal with the waterways of the country, with a view to obtaining a grant from the Government for re-opening the navigation. The canal, as every Ipswichian knows, is already in navigable condition as far as Bramford; and as it is estimated that £2,000 would be sufficient to render the stretch between Bramford and Stowmarket serviceable for barges, it is to be hoped that for the benefit of the trade of Stowmarket and Mid-Suffolk generally that a small sum will be forthcoming. There are already several important industries established at Stowmarket which would welcome the re-opening of the canal, bringing them, as it would, in direct communication with the sea by water carriage; and the establishment of such facilities might attract other manufacturers to Stowmarket, now that they are being driven out of the large towns by excessive rates.

On the 3 May 1907, it was reported that "there was a movement on foot to re-establish a means of communication between Stowmarket and Ipswich and suggested that the canal between Stowmarket and Ipswich should be restored". In 1909, the Evening Star reported the condition of the lock gates were such that they could not be used and it was agreed they should be repaired.

Traffic continued on the Lower reaches as far as Bramford with Fisons and Packard carrying fertiliser to a factory along the river. Soon after the First World War, Fisons ceased to use barges and the last Packard barge was in 1929. The navigation company went bankrupt in 1930 and the Navigation was closed in 1932.

Every year the navigation company held an annual inspection of the waterway. For this purpose, they borrowed a lighter and officials and their wives toured the entire waterway with lunch served on board. They were often supported by locals who would turn out and cheer them on their way. A similar practice was carried out on the Chelmer and Blackwater Navigation every year.

Baylham Lock Gate 1960. RGT Historic Website Image

In 1932, the Trustees resolved formally to close the navigation, and obtained an order permitting it under the Land Drainage Act 1930.

The passing of the Land Drainage Act 1930 meant that they did not need to obtain an Act of Parliament to close the navigation, and instead a closing order was obtained under section 41 of that Act. The Minister of Agriculture and Fisheries confirmed the order on 5 October 1932.

Baylham Lock and gates 1995.
RGT Historic Website Image

A final meeting was held on 16 March 1934, when debts were settled, and the remaining money (£216) was split between East Suffolk County Council and the East Suffolk Rivers Catchment Board, who had responsibility for the river under the terms of the Land Drainage Act. All records were passed to the clerk of the Catchment Board, and the meeting closed with a vote of thanks to the Trustees' own clerk for his commitment over the years.

# 15. The Suffolk Twin

In the December 1979 edition of 'Waterways World', the late John Marriage, a well-known and respected historian wrote an article titled 'Suffolk Twin'. A few excerpts of it are copied below.

The Ipswich and Stowmarket Navigation, together with the Chelmer and the nearby Stour, were three of a group of individually isolated waterways, each running inland from the sea into East Anglia and built in the eighteenth century to allow

the benefits of the coastwide trade to penetrate far inland. These river navigations each had their own particular characteristics, but the Chelmer and Gipping Navigation - to give the latter its more usual title - were uncannily alike. Both ran through quiet, gentle, pastoral East Anglian countryside; both are of similar length (Chelmer 14 miles, Gipping 16 miles) and finally, navigation on works and commercial craft operating on them were almost identical. Indeed, the vessels were different from any other craft elsewhere. These similarities are less surprising when it is realised that John Rennie designed them both, and that both shared the same resident engineer, Richard Coates.

https://magazineexchange.co.uk/cw/waterways-world-magazine-december-1979-issue.html

Springfield Basin, Chelmsford.
Courtesy www.waterways.org.uk

The Chelmer closed during the Second World War but reopened with a fleet of barges transporting timber from Heybridge Basin (where the Chelmer joins the Blackwater estuary) to Chelmsford until 1972, when the navigation moved away from chasing leisure boaters off the waterway to encouraging them, offering moorings and other services.

Today it is a fully maintained waterway welcoming leisure boats, walkers, anglers, joggers, cyclists, canoes, paddle boards and even swimmers.

The Inland Waterways Association's (IWA) subsidiary company, Essex Waterways Ltd took over the management of the Chelmer & Blackwater Navigation in 2005 and carry out regular maintenance work along its length.

It is a living demonstration of what the Gipping could also be like, after all, the two Navigations started out almost identical in design and construction. The only difference with the Chelmer was that it somehow stayed open and in use against all the odds, and residents and local authorities now recognise how valuable it is to have a fully maintained waterway nearby, with Chelmsford City Council actively working on an extension of the navigation with a proposed new lock and bridge.

A canal boat in a lock on the Chelmer
Photo taken by the author

Research shows that being by water is good for you, so having the river teeming with life will help to make us all feel happier and healthier. Waterways are an incredibly valuable asset and research has shown that the restoration of waterways can bring economic, social and environment benefits to an area.

Barge Victoria at Paper Mill, on the Chelmer.
Photo taken by the author

The Government "recognise the very considerable benefits our canal network brings in myriad ways, such as providing greater access to the outdoors, enhancing wellbeing, bringing us closer to water, engaging with nature— those water plantains—increasing leisure and recreation, increasing regeneration and bringing value to the economy."

Essex Waterways boat charters state that; "Much of our wonderful waterway runs through tranquil Essex countryside, and is the perfect place for an afternoon or evening cruise. Charter a boat for your outing or celebration or turn up and buy a ticket for a one hour cruise."
https://waterways.org.uk/waterways/sites/essex-waterways/boat-trips
Chelmer Canal Trust https://www.chelmercanaltrust.co.uk/cct.htm

# 16. Restoration Work along the Navigation

The River Gipping Trust aim is to restore limited navigation along the canal and restore the towpath alongside the canal. Together with the Inland Waterways Association (IWA), the River Gipping Trust has already restored the John Rennie locks of Bosmere, Creeting and Baylham and are working on restoring Pipps Ford lock so that soon all four will be ready, fully restored, awaiting the installation of lock gates.

Of the 15 lock structures built, 14 remain with the river flowing through all of them. The one missing lock is Claydon which was lost during the construction of the A14.

Often reported as being built over, it actually lays between the road and the river, but has been severely damaged and filled in.

Baylham Lock Restoration 2009.
RGT Historic Website Image

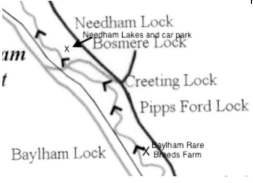

The Trust firstly intend to restore navigation along the 3-mile stretch of the river between the popular Needham Market Lakes and the Rare Breeds Farm and wooden mill at Baylham, creating new recreational and leisure facilities on the river to improve the life and welfare of the area's inhabitants with a trip boat running between the two locations.

With a more consistent depth to the river to allow navigation, the restoration work will enhance biodiversity whilst preserving the historic heritage of the Navigation by restoring the structures that enabled navigation and caring for the flora and fauna of The Gipping Valley.

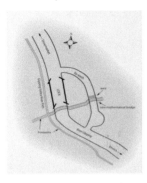

At Pipps Ford, a new by-wash has been created as the old one had completely disappeared with no trace remaining. The by-wash is the channel which allows excess water to flow around a lock. All locks have them. The by-wash is around 200 feet long and 10 feet deep with profiled sides. A new 'Mathematical Bridge' was built across the by-wash. Diagram left shows the by-wash and photo below of the mathematical bridge.

Whilst digging the by-wash, Trust volunteers uncovered the 230-year old brick remains of the original weir, the bricks were all cleaned up and restored and form part of the current weir.

Pipps Ford by-wash, river bridge and mathematical bridge.
Photo taken by the author

The Trust has more recently restored the 230-year old brick footbridge abutments just upstream of Baylham and has constructed a new wooden footbridge platform sitting on top of the abutments. John Rennie's notes have this bridge costed at £102. The abutments were in a very poor condition and the Trust recovered around 500 of the original bricks from the river bed and rebuilt the abutments using these bricks.

The original footbridge platform was last seen in a very sorry state at the bottom of the river in 1942.

The footbridge was an essential part of the original towpath which crossed the river at this point. It enabled the horses pulling the barges to cross over from one side to the other.

The new footbridge reopens a one kilometre long stretch of footpath along the route of the original towpath which was closed to the public for nearly one hundred years.

Brick Abutment Remains 2020. Photo taken by author

River Gipping Trust volunteers celebrating the completion of the wooden footbridge platform and 1793 brick abutment restoration. Photo taken by author

**How will the Gipping look in a few years' time?**

Creeting Lock and Bridge. John Rennie engineered, built by Richard Coates 1793

In a few year's time this is how Creeting lock could look. With lock gates and a lock full of water, just how it was designed 230 years ago.

Lock and bridge on the Chelmer and Blackwater Navigation in Essex. John Rennie engineered, built by Richard Coates 1797. Both photos taken by author

# 17. John Rennie's Legacy

As well as around ten lock structures there remains a few bridges. There were around 20 bridges built to Rennie's design of which all his recorded estimates remain. Probably the best is at Creeting and Baylham, both of which have their lock and bridges Grade II listed.

Above; Creeting Lock and bridge. The 1930s photo was taken when it was known as Bosmere lower mill when the mill still existed. Historic England have Creeting Lock and bridge listed as a Grade II listed building. Described as; 1793. John Rennie, engineer. Red brick with stone and dressing to lock.

Maybe this is the oldest John Rennie engineered bridge still in existence
https://historicengland.org.uk/listing/the-list/list-entry/1261325
RGT Historic Website Image (top). Photo above taken by the author

An early and more recent photo of Baylham lock and bridge.

Both locks are crying out for lock gates to be installed. All 12 locks with working lock gates on the Chelmer and Blackwater Navigation in Essex are Grade II listed. The locks and bridges on the Gipping are around 4 years older, only two are listed and look identical to the John Rennie designed bridges on the Chelmer and Blackwater Navigation.

RGT Website. John Jarman Postcard collection (top), photo above by the author

# 18. Locks along the Ipswich to Stowmarket Canal

By 1793, there were 15 locks constructed and operational between Ipswich and Stowmarket. Three of these, between Needham Market and Stowmarket, were William Jessop engineered, built of turf and timber construction and were completed in 1791. Each of these had brick built vertical walls to support the lock gates, but in-between the gates were sloping earth banks which necessitated a much longer filling and emptying time. The other twelve locks are John Rennie engineered, built between 1792 and 1793 of brick and stone construction.

Stowupland Lock. The first turf and timber lock on the navigation. Completely destroyed and replaced by a concrete structure and a flood control system, with no by-wash or bypass weir. Probably a complete rebuild would be required to enable navigation to be restored through this lock.

Badley Lock. The second turf and timber lock, restored in 1948 to its original design. This lock is of tremendous historical importance being one of only four in the whole country. It is now in poor order with trees growing through the structure and is in danger of complete collapse. It is in private ownership and it is understood the landowner is opposed to any work being done. Could be fully restored with some timber uprights being replaced.

Needham Lock. The third turf and timber lock. Rebuilt with a flood control lifting gate at a rebuilt entrance. The sloping earth banks remain together with the tail brickwork that supported the bottom gates. Not too much work needed to restore it to navigation.

Bosmere Lock. Possibly the first and oldest John Rennie lock on the canal, indeed in the whole country and the first to be fully restored (apart from lock gates). No major works required, just lock gates to be installed.

Creeting Lock. (Riverside Farm). The second fully restored lock (apart from lock gates). Both lock and bridge are Grade II listed as being engineered by John Rennie. No major works required, just lock gates to be installed.

Pipps Ford Lock. Originally named Pool House Lock. Currently under restoration by the River Gipping Trust. The by-wash has been restored. No major works required. It needs to have the capability of stop plank installation and then lock gates installed.

Baylham Lock. Another Grade II listed lock and bridge. No major work is needed. Fully restored ready for lock gates to be installed.

Shamford Lock. Restored many years ago but with lock gate recesses in the wrong place and the wrong size with no by-wash. This lock will need a partial rebuild to re-align the gate recesses along with the excavation of a new by-wash to divert water around the lock.

Blakenham Lock. This lock appears to be in good condition, but it is wholly within private property. No major works required.

Claydon Lock. This lock was lost during the construction of the A14. One lock chamber wall remains buried between the river and the A14, but no evidence can be found of the other chamber wall. Possibly this wall was demolished and buried in the lock chamber. The old lock position lays between the diverted new river course and the A14, with a footpath around it. Either a new lock needs to be built (space is available) or, if sufficient remains of the old lock can be found, it could hopefully be partially restored. A new by-wash will be required, but possibly the current 'new' river could be used.

Paper Mill Lock. This lock appears to be in good condition but has a lifting gate for flood control which would likely have to be incorporated into any works on the lock.

Bramford Lock. The Environment Agency and Anglian Water have some major works around this lock which would interfere with a fully restored lock. Depending upon how significant these works are and their possible need to be relocated could make this a significant project, but work on the lock itself is not thought to be major.

Sproughton Lock. This lock appears to be in good condition. It has a lifting gate for flood control which would likely have to be incorporated into any works on the lock. A new by-wash might be needed.

Chantry Lock. This lock seems to have been destroyed and replaced with a concrete structure. It too has a lifting gate for flood control. This lock would seem to need a complete rebuild.

Handford Tide Lock. This is the last lock on the river and the largest, around twice the width of the other locks along the canal. It was constructed to maintain the canal levels no matter what the state of the tidal Orwell was. It is a massive structure but appears to be in good condition with built in flood control equipment. Although not impossible to restore, it would be hard to justify with high investment and running costs and little benefit.

# 19. Some Historic John Rennie Lock Images

Bosmere Lock and Mill with Cart Lodge. RGT Historic Website Image

Creeting Lock, Bridge and Florence Ward c.1930. RGT Historic Website Image

Baylham Lock around 1890. RGT Historic Website Image

Shamford Lock 1905. RGT Website. John Jarman Postcard collection

Blakenham Lock and Mill. RGT Historic Website Image

Blakenham Lock 1908. RGT Website. John Jarman Postcard collection

Claydon Lock (lost during A14 construction). RGT Historic Website Image

Claydon Lock and Bridge around 1890. RGT Historic Website Image

Bramford Lock. RGT Website. John Jarman Postcard collection

Bramford Lock. RGT Historic Website Image

Sproughton Lock. RGT Website. John Jarman Postcard collection

Sproughton Lock 1913. RGT Website. John Jarman Postcard collection

Thought to be Chantry Lock. RGT Historic Website Image

Handford Sea Lock. RGT Website. John Jarman Postcard collection

# 20. The Gipping Meets the Orwell

The River Gipping meets the River Orwell in two places. Until the navigational demise and the loss of the Handford sea lock, barges up to 55ft could navigate from the River Orwell into the Gipping.

For much of the history of the town, the east channel (right channel on map) was called the Gipping, to reflect its fresh water content. The western channel is referred to as the Orwell, as seawater flows up to the north end of the island.

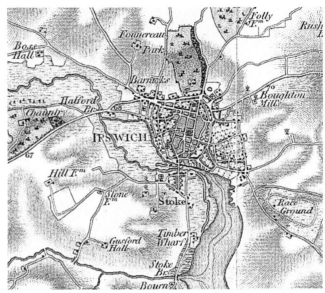

Pre-1842 Map (courtesy visionofbritain.org.uk)

The main (west) channel flowing down the middle of the valley is often delineated 'The salt water'. The more easterly channel (the Gipping) is said to be clearly artificial, and of great antiquity: it already existed in AD970. Archaeologists have found a Roman settlement beside it, and the channel may have been excavated during the Roman occupation of Britain.

Note the map refers to Handford Bridge as 'Halford Bridge', Chantry Park as 'Chauntry' and Christchurch Park as 'Fonnereau Park'.

Boss Hall rail viaduct 1901. RGT Historic Website Image

Rowing Boat Hire Below Boss Hall 1913.
RGT Website. John Jarman postcard collection

IMT Image Archive. Ipswich Town Marshes and Gipping c.1850. David Kindred Collection

Just upstream of Handford Lock lies an old part of the Alderman Canal. In the past, a further section of the Gipping existed, sometimes referred to as the "Little" or "Upper" Gipping, possibly a man-made cut which flowed east from the Gipping, before turning south-east, to rejoin the River Orwell at Stoke Bridge. Only a section of this canal now remains, known as Alderman Canal East, a 1.6 hectare Local Nature Reserve and Alderman Canal West, a one hectare Local Nature Reserve.

At the east end of this stretch of water, close to Handford Road was Handford Mill (see chapter 11). This was a water-powered mill believed originally to have been fed by a stream, possibly dug by the Romans to bring water to a mill near the site of Handford Mill (the first written record of which is found

IMT Image Archive. Alderman Canal c1890. Leonard Woolf Collection

as early as the 13th century). The channel was known to exist when the bounds of Stoke were made in AD970. A valve now prevents flow between the River Gipping and Alderman Canal. Today a flood control barrier built into the upper end of Handford Lock chamber (located by West End Bridge) maintains the river at a reasonably constant level but fails to attract leisure users.

Handford Sea Lock viewed from West End Bridge.
Photo taken by the author

There is evidence of earlier rowing boat hire, canoes, a rowing club, a sailing school and wild water swimmers in this area.

## The Ipswich to Stowmarket Navigation – John Rennie's First Canal Project

There were many failed attempts to connect the Gipping to the Orwell further downstream at the Wet Dock below Stoke Bridge, in effect extending the canal. In 1841, prior to construction of the Wet Dock, a voluminous report was produced by the Dock engineer detailing the merits etc. of a connection and the report was considered by the Trustees of the Stowmarket Navigation who supported the report and stated their willingness to contribute a moderate sum towards its implementation.

Another attempt was made in 1875, when plans were drawn up to improve dock access to the navigation. It's not clear if this would have eliminated the need for Handford lock, or if, the proposed dam and weir were to be of half-tide design as per the current weir near the Bobby Robson Bridge. The stopping of the tidal flow in the New Cut was very contentious (as it is today) and was fiercely opposed by many, but made it into the bill on the grounds there was no obligation to carry out the work….. and it wasn't.

Courtesy British Newspaper Archive

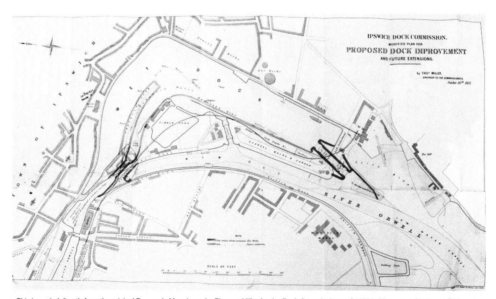

This is copied directly from the original Proposals Map drawn by Thomas Miller for the Dock Commissioners in 1875. His proposals were radical, and included (in pink) a weir across the New Cut (in front of the present day Stoke Quay buildings) and a lock to give direct access for Stowmarket Navigation barges into the River Gipping under Stoke Bridge. This would have resulted in water in the Gipping remaining at a high level above the new weir at all states of the tide. A complementary proposal, in green, was for a cargo transfer 'finger' wharf in the middle of the dock. In the event, these elements of the Proposals were never implemented. His second major proposal was for the new lock at the southern end of the dock giving easier passage for sailing vessels approaching and leaving the dock, and a new quay along the western side of the dock, then a shelving beach.

Courtesy Ipswich Maritime Trust
With IMT own wording and interpretation of the IDC proposal

*Bob Malster, in his book 'A Victorian Vision – The Building of Ipswich Wet Dock' writes*

Alarm bells sounded in 1836 when the Trustees read of proposals to build an enclosed dock at Ipswich. They realised that the positioning of the proposed lock would mean that vessels from Stowmarket would be unable to enter the dock directly from the river. They would first have to proceed downriver past the lock entrance, before turning round to sail back upstream into the dock.

What they wanted was a second small lock at the north end of the dock to provide a short-cut for barges coming down from Stowmarket, or leaving the dock to proceed up the navigation. They even offered, in an eleventh-hour letter to the Dock Commissioners in June 1841, to contribute a moderate sum "to meet the expenses attending its accomplishment". Their entreaties fell on deaf ears, and the new dock was completed the following year with a single entrance that faced downstream.

Bargeowners who attended a meeting of the Trustees of the navigation in February 1842 complained that the new lock was regularly causing them to lose a tide. Whereas they had formerly been able to reach the quays at Ipswich, discharge their cargo and return on the same tide, they were now often forced to wait until the next tide before they could

A photo by Robert Burrows, taken around 1850, probably the oldest photo of a Gipping lock, Burrows is top-hatted, as usual in his photos. He possibly took the oldest Gipping barge photo too, (chapter 12 refers). Probably Handford lock.
Courtesy Suffolk Archives (Ipswich) K485/Plate 96
https://www.suffolkarchives.co.uk

return to Stowmarket. Even when they were able to leave the dock on the same tide, they could not get up to the first river lock at Handford Bridge because of the fast-ebbing tide. They also complained that the still water of the dock was sometimes frozen over before ice blocked their canal - perhaps a sign that the climate was more severe 150 years ago. Problems such as these paled into insignificance when, in 1845, an Act was obtained and approved for the building of a railway between Ipswich and Stowmarket.

# 21. Wright and Sons Boat Builders

With grateful contributions from Bob (Richard) Pawsey, Ipswich Maritime Trust and Eric's two daughters Jennifer Beckett and Gillian Rowe from Canada

"It is worth recording a brief and untold history of the Wright's boat building business in Cullingham Road. In the first instance, c1900, Ellis J Wright, who was a stonemason by trade, (we know this from an entry in the 1904 Kelly's directory) became the proprietor of the King William public house at 141 London Road and rented out rowing boats from the pub gardens which backed onto the River Gipping. Initially two boats were purchased from a Thames boatyard and were a great success. Then his eldest son, born in 1886, James Garrod, known as Gary, became involved together with a brother, George C, who was seven years younger. First though, Gary followed in his father's footsteps by taking on stonemasonry and is registered in Kelly's 1916 as working from 74 Cullingham Road. It is interesting to note that Ellis and his wife Emma had seven sons and two daughters by the time Emma was 39, (a family size quite normal for those days).

Gary, a shrewd operator, realised that the boats needed maintenance and so acquired the freehold of the site number 72 at the far end of Cullingham Road and created the business of Wright & Son (Ipswich) Ltd. This site was complete with a large shed and outbuildings

Cullingham Road Boat Building

which had been used by a furniture manufacturer. It is known from Alison Wright in New Zealand that Gary and brother George took one of their rowing boats to pieces, plank by plank to see how it was constructed and so commenced to build boats. Gary married in 1913 and their first son, Jack was born in 1914 and Eric followed in 1915.

The business was handed over to Eric and Jack, his brother in 1935 when Eric was twenty years old due to Gary's ill health. However, Jack was not interested and went off to pursue his own career becoming a prominent electrical engineer; (Jack's son, Peter became a well-known nuclear engineer). This left Eric to build the business by increasing the range of boats quite dramatically with the help of Kim Holman, a yacht designer.

The basic range of boats designed by Kim Holman and Eric, as listed in the Wright's catalogue, included 6' to 10' pram dinghies, stem dinghies 6' to 10', rowing boats, skiffs, canoes and sailing dinghies. At this point, just take a look at the price of a 6' pram dinghy; £5 8s 0d (£5.40) complete with galvanised rowlocks and spruce oars, carriage paid to any railway station in the mainland!

The range of sailing craft started with open, gaff rigged, centre board dinghies 8' to 16'. This was as well as renting a fleet of rowing boats from the slipway behind the works. Rowers could row upstream to Yarmouth Road Bridge where they used a bypass and hauled the boats over rollers because of a flood control sluice immediately against the upstream side of the bridge. Once over the rollers and back into the river it was possible to row to Sproughton and on to Bramford. It wasn't possible to turn left after the Yarmouth Road bridge to go down the River Orwell under the Seven Arches bridge as there was a series of cascading pools or rather weirs (now replaced by a sluice and banks lined with steel piling). Today, you can still see the bypass, although it has been reduced in width due to an extra re-inforcing brick pier for the bridge, and the bypass has mostly been filled in. The sluice against the upstream side of Yarmouth Road Bridge has been removed and the canalised Gipping is now open.

Displaying at the London Boat Show

In the last quarter of 1939, Eric married Hilda McNamara, whose father was the owner of the well-known Ipswich firm of McNamara Motors.

During the War, Eric won tenders to supply the War Department with different types of small wooden craft. Amongst the range of sailing craft built by the yard were the Twinkle 10 and Twinkle 12 centreboard, three quarter decked, sailing dinghies designed by Francis Jones. Mahogany clinker planked, on oak frames and copper fastened; a Twinkle 12 which came with a suit of Egyptian cotton sails and a pair of varnished oars with leather rowlock protectors and copper reinforced blades, ready to sail, would have cost £125, c1956. Other classes of sailing craft included a 14' centre board Weekender, another Francis Jones design. A larger craft was the 22' Kestrel, a centreboard yacht with deck stepped mast, again designed by Francis Jones which was built to order for customers.

Eric supplied wholesale quantities of dinghies to other boatyards all over the country, as well as direct retail sales. These would be delivered by road on special trailers with the boats stacked upright. Another avenue of business was the supply of paddle boats to Amusement Parks, again built to customers' requirements from all over the country. Showing at the London Boat Show brought in many enquiries. Eric was unique in the boat-building industry in that he didn't lay off staff for the winter months but kept building for stock and by the time the season started would have several hundred boats in stock. Thus, he could deliver immediately and at keen prices. Not only that but it meant his staff turnover was very low.

Of worthy note is that Wright & Son (Ipswich) Ltd, were the first company to exhibit a fibreglass boat at The London Boat Show.

A Wright Paddle Boat

Eric was not only enterprising but was a skilled craftsman in his own right. It is remembered that he would not allow anyone but himself to use a spindle moulder machine for making jigs as it was so easy for the operator to lose fingers and hands. He is also remembered for his passion for jigs and machines which reduced his requirement for labour. However, although Eric was very industrious in his business affairs, he did not get on well with his son, John, a gifted boatbuilder, who eventually decided to emigrate to New Zealand with his wife Alison. John and Alison with their four sons built their own successful distribution and haulage business empire in New Zealand. Wrights eventually ceased trading in 1972". It is reported that there was sailing on the River Gipping up to the 1950s.

Jersey Heritage have a printed and typed pro-forma invoice from Wright & Son (Ipswich) Ltd dated 10th December 1945 for the building of a 12' standard yacht dinghy for £41-19s-6d.

A few words should be told about Eric Wright's part in the creation of Levington Marina (although it has no direct connection with the River Gipping). In the Spring of 1967, there were 6 original investors: Michael Spear, Eric Wright, John Adams, Chris Carter Jonas, Kim Holman and the farmer, George Stennet who owned the land. Each provided capital and their own expertise to dig out some of the marshes to form a yacht basin. Over the years, it has expanded using its own capital to the vast enterprise it is today and is the leading independent marina on the East Coast. The whole story is told elsewhere in a booklet and is an interesting read.

Before we leave boat building on the River Gipping, it should be mentioned that a small enterprise set up in the old timber framed stables behind the Royal William Inn in London Road. This was much later and was run by Dennis Elvin who, when he left the Austin Farrar Woolverstone Shipyard as an apprentice when it closed in 1954, started building "Gipping Prams" of marine plywood and clinker dinghies built to order. The business ceased when the stables burnt down. After various changes of name, the inn itself was eventually demolished and is now the site of the Lidl Supermarket.

In a 2009 edition of the Ipswich Star, written by David Kindred, it reported that; Robert Sheppard's mother Vera (nee Powell), "has very fond memories of working for a boat-builder Wright and Sons of Cullingham Road, from the mid 1930s until 1950…. The business was then run by Gary Wright and his son Eric. Gary Wright's parents owned the Royal William public house on London Road and when he was young Gary spent his time on the riverbank close to the Royal William making small boats"….. "This must have been the beginnings of his business. He hired out boats for a few pence on a Sunday".

Wendy Orris (nee Thrower), said: "As I studied the picture of rowing boats lined up along the tow path, I was suddenly back in 1947. "My first husband and I hired a boat from the Royal William public house in London Road and had an idyllic few hours on the water, resulting in our getting engaged after pulling into the bank".

A Twinkle 10 under sail with crew and a few other Twinkle 12 and 10s on the River Gipping around 1950. IMT Image Archive. David Kindred Collection

## Twinkle sailing dinghies built by Wright's

There are still many clinker-built Twinkle sailing dinghies around, with reasonable examples of 12s fetching upwards of £2,000 (compare that with an earlier price new of £125). Most are advertised as being built by Wright and Son (Ipswich) Ltd during the 1950s and 1960s.

Twinkle 12s (TT) racing at Overy Staithe S.C.
Courtesy Overy Staithe Sailing Club www.overystaithesc.org.uk

The Twinkle 10 was said to make an ideal yacht tender for a classic sailing or motor yacht, and an excellent boat for the family to learn and enjoy sailing in true Swallows and Amazons' style. They sail very well, are well rigged and can be quite exciting in strong winds.

There is also a Facebook group page called *"Twinkle 10', 12' and family 14' Wright and Sons boatbuilders"*, with many photos (past and present), lots of restoration projects and the odd 'Wright' boat for sale. There is a lovely photo of a Twinkle 10 named 'Dolphin' which has been in the same family since 1968 and kept at Overy Staithe together with another five Twinkle 10s.

Overy Staithe sailing club in Norfolk is recognised as Wright boats spiritual homeland with a good mix of 10s, 12s and 14s, many participating in club races with the 14s on a PY (handicap) of  1214.

# 22.River Bathing Places and Swimming Clubs

Both Ipswich and Stowmarket swimming clubs have ties to the river Gipping.

Stowmarket had a purpose built river bathing place which was the foundation stone of the creation of Stowmarket Swimming Cub in 1888. A dam was built to create a pool in the River Rat at Woodfield Lane, around 500 metres upstream from it's outlet into the River Gipping.

It was a very popular pool, known locally as the Bathing Place and was open all year round, even on Christmas Day. The pool bottom had to be cleaned of mud every few years to make it more pleasant for swimmers.

The demise of the Bathing Place occurred with the opening of an open air Swimming Pool in 1937 off Ipswich Road, which itself was very popular until closed in 1985. Stowmarket Swimming Club still thrives today and have been at the indoor Mid Suffolk Leisure centre since 1986.

Ipswich Swimming Club was founded in 1884 and its members in 1909 had reduced admission rates into the river Gipping's fresh water West End Bathing Place.

The Evening Star reported on two bathing places along the Gipping and Orwell rivers on 18 June 1909.

"Two open-air bathing places, one over Stoke of salt water from the Orwell and the West End Bathing Place of fresh water from the Gipping. That at Stoke was constructed so long ago as 1843, and has undoubtedly been a great blessing to the town. It used to be much more extensively patronised than of late years - that is to say, before the Orwell had the sewage of the town discharged into it. The water nowadays is however, very clean and has the advantage of being salt, which many prefer.

The place is let to Mr F V Martin, whose charges are the same as for the West End Bathing Place, namely from threepence to a penny, with a large part free. There are plenty of bathing boxes and diving facilities; there is a deep and a shallow end, and a boat is kept afloat constantly in case of emergency.

The West End Bathing Place is in the hands of the Corporation, who place an attendant in charge. This place is well maintained and is a popular resort on summer mornings before breakfast. It was constructed in 1823, the space it occupies being excavated from land beside the Gipping. It has a concrete bottom, the depth being from three to ten feet, and while for threepence the bather can have a private box, a bath can be had for a penny from a shed, and there is also some Free water.

The members of the Ipswich Swimming Club or any other recognised club have season tickets at a reduced price at both bathing places, and anyone can purchase for five shillings a season ticket, available from May 1st to September 30th. The baths are open from 6 am. to sunset on week days and from 6 am. to 10 am. on Sundays. The West End Bathing Place is reserved for ladies now on Wednesdays from 3 pm. to sunset, and on Friday mornings from 9 am. to 1 pm.

A ladies section of the Ipswich Swimming Club has this summer been formed. The Education Committee send a lot of their Elementary school children to both places to be taught. The boys are taught by members of the Swimming Club, classes of fifteen boys being made up. The Swimming Club receives an honorarium for this useful work. In the case of the girls, Miss Palmer gives the instruction. The number of bathers at the West End Bathing Place in the course of a month varies from 2,600 to 6,000, according to the weather and about four-fifths of those using the bath go free".

In 1938, the Broomhill Open Air Swimming Pool on Sherrington Road opened. Around half a mile from the West End Bathing Pool on the Gipping, it had heated water to 21c and a grandstand for 700 spectators.

The Modern style pool building is one of the most attractive Lido style open-air pools in Britain and is one of the deepest with the highest outdoor diving board. It is now one of only 17 Grade II listed Lidos in Britain.

Ipswich Swimming Club is now known as TeamIpswich Swimming, the club primarily trains at Crown Pools, Ipswich.

# 23. Ipswich Waterfront – A gift from Henry VIII

Ipswich sits at the junction of the lowest crossing of the Orwell and the head of navigation for seagoing vessels. Reported as possibly the oldest of all English ports, with an almost continuous record of maritime trading activity, since about the year 600.

Gipping barges at Stoke Bridge
IMT Image Archive. Gipping barges c.1890. Harry Walters Collection

Ipswich is where it is because of the river – it developed where the fresh water of the River Gipping meets the salt water of the River Orwell. It therefore gave dual benefits of access to fresh drinking water for townspeople while maintaining proximity to the coast and the waters beyond.

From early Saxon settlers and Viking invasions, to global maritime trade and luxury yacht building; the Waterfront has been the at the heart of Ipswich's transformations over the town's 1,500-year history. Ipswich Waterfront is one of the most recognisable areas of the town, popular for the many bars, cafes and bistros perched along the water's edge, and with views over the marinas.

The quayside was a Hanseatic Headport (a medieval Northern Europe commercial and defensive confederation between the 13th and 15th centuries). It was a hub of commercial and social activity through the Middle Ages. The wealth of timbered buildings and churches that survive in town were funded by this trade. Plague and the decline of the wool trade in the 17th century contributed to some 200 years of slow economic and population growth. The free rights to the Orwell were granted by Henry VIII to the residents of Ipswich as a reward for Cardinal Wolsey's services, but have been largely lost.

IMT Image Archive. Packard Navigation Barge in Ipswich Lock c.1890.
Leonard Woolf collection

There was a medieval marsh located South West of the town between Stoke and Handford bridges. This extensive waterlogged land provided a natural defence for the town, making it very difficult to launch an attack on foot or on horseback.

The river itself provided a defence, too. We have to imagine the river as much broader and shallower around the original fording point used by the Anglo-Saxons (and probably the Romans before them) from Great Whip Street in the south and Foundry Lane in the north.

In 991, a fleet of 93 Viking ships swept up the River Orwell and sacked the town.

The Ipswich Dock Act, the first act to be signed by the new Queen Victoria in 1837, allowed the New Cut to be dug; the gates of the biggest wet dock in the country opened in 1842 and the area was a hive of industry up until the 1970s, at the time of completion, the dock was known as 'the biggest and most important enclosed dock in the kingdom'.

Then came the railway in 1846. Over the next 40 years the dock and railways fed an economic bonanza lasting until the decline of manufacturing in the 1970s. The river is said to be cleaner now than at any time in the past 200 years.

River Orwell – IMT Image Archive. Leonard Woolf Collection

The New Cut was a major transport route for pleasure steamers in the 19th and early-20th centuries. The Steamboat Inn survives. The landing stages for the steamers have rotted, though pontoons remain for Debbage's yard and the Ipswich Rowing Club.

# Appendix - A Transcript of John Rennie's Notes

John Rennie kept notes of most of the letters he wrote and these are kept at The National Library of Scotland. His notes on the Gipping have been transcribed by the River Gipping Trust and are reproduced below:

London December 20th 1791

To the Trustees for directing the Works on the Stowmarket Navigation

In company with J Grigsby Esq and the Revd Mr H Hill I took an Eye Survey of the River Gippen from Stowmarket to Ipswich on the 13th, 14th & 15th instant and made such observations and enquiries relative to the works now executing including any to be done as appearing to me to be proper for enabling me to form a plan for the further guidance of the Trustees in the conduct of said works.

From Stowmarket to Needham the works are nearly finished but in several places it will be necessary to make considerable alterations.

In the First Place I recommend the puddling the additional Land Tyes to the Timber Locks now executed at Crofts Mill; the Gates also to be put in proper condition.

Secondly, to take away the weir at the Tail of said Mill and to make a small Cut to carry the water from the Mill Tail further down to come out into the navigable part of the River in as easy an inclination as possible. To deepen its bottom gradually from near the Mill Tail to the River and to widen the New Cut at its entrance so that the water may join the River with a gentle motion. By this means you will avoid the inconvenience of having a Bank of Soil always raised at the Junction of the two waters as is now the case. The same should be done at Badley Mill.

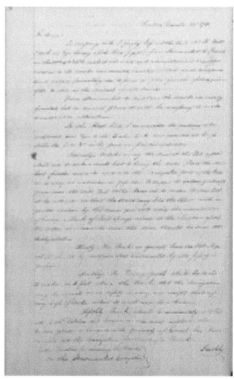

Copy of John Rennie's original 1791 note to the Navigation Company

Thirdly, the Banks in general have too little Slope which should be rectified – that recommended by Mr Jessop is proper.

Fourthly – The Towing path should be raised 18 inches or 2 feet above the Banks, that the Navigation may be carried on in safety in every case except that of very high floods, when it must cease for a time.

Fifthly - Trunks should be immediately end laid into such Ditches and Drains as are now without them. In one place a considerable quantity of Gravel has been carried into the Navigation for want of a Trunk.

Sixthly, Occupation and Road Bridges should immediately be executed where the Navigation Works are nearly finished. In general, where the ground is low you cannot do better than make such as the Swing Bridge at Croft's Mill for small roads and fixed Timber Bridges for large ones such as Mr Jessop has drawn. In public Roads, Brick Bridges are preferable.

Having stated some general observations in respect of the works now in hand, I shall next give my opinion on those that are to be executed. In every work it is a wise maxim to lay down a proper plan on the first outset and to pursue the same with diligence afterwards. In this case the general outlines previous to obtaining the Acts of Parliament seems to have been well pointed out by Mr Jessop but the proper steps to be pursued afterwards have been neglected. A regular Survey of the River should have been taken and the works to be executed properly laid down.

The original Survey is very incorrect. I am surprised Mr Lenny should have paid so little attention to accuracy – this makes it necessary to set about a new Survey as to lay down the true form of the River with the different works to be proposed. The Side Cuts should be laid down and the places of the Locks marked out. When this is completed the ground for the foundation of the Locks should be bored which will enable me to point out the proper mode of laying down the foundation of each.

I would advise that the three timber locks now executed should stand, but the others to be done of Brick, plenty of which I doubt not will be found in the course of the proposed Navigation - at least if earth cannot be had of a sufficient good quality to make front Bricks it may be for those that are used in doing the Back or Inside parts of the Lock Walls and good ones may be furnished for the face

Timber Locks from being exposed so frequently to Wet and Dry in the chamber and the Side next the ground being constantly damp soon decay and will in time injure much to the Navigation and Mills.

Messrs Grigsby & Hill have given directions to search for bricks and I hope the rest of the Trustees will accordingly join them in preparing a sufficiency to proceed with expedition on the Locks and other works against next Spring.

# The Ipswich to Stowmarket Navigation – John Rennie's First Canal Project

I have carefully looked at the place on the River Orwell where the barges are intended to be admitted into the Tideway and I have examined the subject as far as the state of the Tides and other local circumstances would permit. The top of the Springs on the 10th inst night the full stream. The observations were made the 15th when the Tide should have been considerably lower but owing to the winds and other causes this was not the case. At the top of the tide which was about 3 o'clock in the afternoon it was measured at the same time and since both at the Custom House Quay, Stoke Bridge and the place where the New Cut is made, it was 8ft 4 at the quay, 7ft at Stoke Bridge and about the same above and from various measurements taken at different times it fell pretty equally at all the three places. In such Tides as these I hesitate not to affirm the place chosen by Mr Jessop is preferable to any other but as I am informed the tides frequently do not flow more than two feet at Stoke Bridge in Neaps and are so weak as to make little or no rise at the proposed Lock and of consequence prevent the Barges from getting into the Navigation which will be a very great injury to the trade of the countryside.

In such cases no doubt Navigation along the Mill Streams and locking to the Orwell just above the Bridge would be preferable although I do not think very much so because 2 feet of water under Stoke Bridge would not be adequate to float a loaded Barge and I am of the opinion that the Orwell may be so deepened to make as much water at the Lock even in these tides as at the bridge and consequently render this place equal to the other and at less expense. I pay no regard to the Argument that has been used in favour of the Locking into the Orwell at the bridge. I mean that the tideway if cleared would soon silt up. The Slightest examination will convince any discerning person that little fear need be entertained on that head.

I must confess if the boats could be admitted into the Tideway near the flood or Water Gates of Mr Rainbird's Mill it would be the best place as thereby a small addition of 16 inches of water would on all Tides be procured and I doubt not such a Plan might be carried into execution at no very great extra Expense. It is possible some opposition might arise from the Incorporation of Ipswich. It would be well this should be enquired into. I also recommend an enquiry to be made relative to Stoke Bridge whether 16 inches could be sunk under the Centre of the Middle Arch. If this could be done and the Orwell deepened so much it would in great measure supersede the necessity of the other.

These, with an Estimate of the Expense of Deepening the Orwell Mr Smith can make out and send me. Mr S should also be directed to observe the low Neaps mentioned above to see whether the information furnished me is just, for from several circumstances I am not inclined to place implicit faith therein. The above information being furnished it will be an easy matter to settle the place of Junction. In the meantime, the Gravel should be taken out of the Orwell to repair such parts of the Banks as are likely to give way. The Trustees having done some work in them are liable to make good the damage by the overflowing of tides.

In the future conduct of these works you must have some person who understands Brick making, Brick Locks and Bridges with the proper composition of Mortar. As for your present Resident Engineer I doubt not is inadequate thereto and it will be very necessary that such a person should carry with him that kind of authority to ensure the execution of the works as directed for without authority there is no certainty of things being properly done. Such a person I shall endeavour, although I cannot absolutely promise, to find.

I beg leave to Submit to the Trustees the necessity of adhering strictly to directions given which will be conformable to the powers granted in the Act of Parliament for if Millers and other persons in the line are to meet with such accommodation as their own humour and convenience require it will be impossible ever to make a complete navigation suited to the purposes of public utility. I do not mean to insinuate that no attention should be paid to Millers and Landowners but only that the general line of navigation should be pursued without suffering any alterations or encroachments to the injury thereof.

I am very respectfully
Your most humble servant
(Signed) John Rennie

PS I shall send you a person to make the Survey above mentioned in February or March next and I shall allow for a few days myself to see matter put in a proper train.

Mr Coates estimate of the Expense of finishing the Stowmarket Navigation. The 3 upper locks and most of the works being finished from Stow-market to Needham

April 16 1792

His notes then include 10 pages of detailed estimates of which this is one page A total of £12,762-8s-3d. This includes the building of 12 locks and around 20 bridges including finishing off three bridges already started at Needham Market.

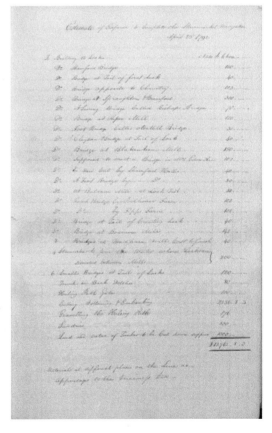

# Acknowledgments

Illustrations and content sources have been acknowledged where possible and we humbly apologise in advance for any errors or omissions and will be happy to correct and acknowledge in any future reprints when advised in writing.

- Civil Engineering Heritage: In East Anglia
  By Peter Cross-Rudkin

- Stowmarket Navigation – Peter Cross-Rudkin.
  https://rbt.org.uk/john-rennie/projects/stowmarket-navigation/

- The Life and Works of John Rennie.
  https://rbt.org.uk/john-rennie/projects/

- The Canals of Eastern England
  by John Boyes, Ronald Russell 1977

- A Biographical Dictionary of Civil Engineers in Great Britain
  and Ireland, edited by A. W. Skempton

- Waterways World, December 1979 edition of The Chelmer's
  Suffolk Twin, by John Marriage

- Ipswich Maritime Trust https://ipswichmaritimetrust.org.uk

- John Jarman postcard collection photos

- Chelmer Canal Trust History By John Marriage.
  http://www.chelmercanaltrust.co.uk/cbhist.htm

- Roman Roads in Britain by David Ratledge
  http://www.twithr.co.uk/suffolk/suffolk.html

- Wikipedia River Gipping. https://en.wikipedia.org/wiki/River_Gipping

- Wikipedia John Rennie the Elder.
  https://en.wikipedia.org/wiki/John_Rennie_the_Elder

- Institution of Civil Engineers.
  https://www.ice.org.uk/news-and-insight/latest-ice-news/ice-john-rennie-commemorative-project

- The Old Lawnmower Club. https://www.oldlawnmowerclub.co.uk

- Newspaper clips courtesy of British Newspaper Archive.
  https://www.britishnewspaperarchive.co.uk

BLAKENHAM.

RGT Website. John Jarman Postcard collection

Great Blakenham Mill and Bridge
RGT Website. John Jarman Postcard collection

Packard Barges Below Turners Tannery
RGT Website. John Jarman Postcard collection